Ian Miller

Inspector of Reformatory Schools of Ireland

twenty-ninth report

Ian Miller

Inspector of Reformatory Schools of Ireland
twenty-ninth report

ISBN/EAN: 9783742800237

Manufactured in Europe, USA, Canada, Australia, Japa

Cover: Foto ©Thomas Meinert / pixelio.de

Manufactured and distributed by brebook publishing software
(www.brebook.com)

Ian Miller

Inspector of Reformatory Schools of Ireland

TWENTY-NINTH REPORT

OF THE

INSPECTOR

APPOINTED TO VISIT THE

REFORMATORY AND INDUSTRIAL SCHOOLS

OF

IRELAND.

CERTIFIED UNDER THE 21ST AND 22ND VIC., CAP. 103; 31ST AND 32ND VIC., CAP. 59;
AND 31ST VIC., CAP. 28.

Presented to both Houses of Parliament by Command of Her Majesty.

DUBLIN:
PRINTED FOR HER MAJESTY'S STATIONERY OFFICE
BY
ALEXANDER THOM & CO. (LIMITED),
And to be purchased, either directly or through any Bookseller, from
HODGES, FIGGIS, and Co., 104, Grafton-street, Dublin; or
EYRE and SPOTTISWOODE, East Harding-street, Fleet-street, E.C.; or
JOHN MENZIES & Co., 12, Hanover-street, Edinburgh; and
88 and 90, West Nile-street, Glasgow.

1891.

CONTENTS.

TWENTY-NINTH REPORT

OF THE

INSPECTOR

OF

REFORMATORY AND INDUSTRIAL SCHOOLS IN IRELAND.

TO THE

RIGHT HON. ARTHUR JAMES BALFOUR, P.C., M.P., &c., &c.,

CHIEF SECRETARY TO THE LORD LIEUTENANT OF IRELAND.

OFFICE OF INSPECTOR OF REFORMATORY AND INDUSTRIAL SCHOOLS IN IRELAND,
DUBLIN CASTLE,

June 9th, 1891.

SIR,

1. I have the honour to submit the Twenty-ninth Report on Reformatory and Industrial Schools in Ireland. It deals with their working and management during the year 1890.

2. I became the head of this Department last autumn, and soon afterwards received the unwelcome news that Mr. Hoope, who had managed the Industrial School at Artane from its foundation, was about to retire from office. That event has since occurred, and as Artane is now the largest institution of its kind in Europe, and a model of organization, I propose, before noticing the Reformatory and Industrial Schools generally, to take a rapid glance at its history from the day it came into existence till it ceased to be governed by the man to whose administrative talent its success is mainly due.

ARTANE INDUSTRIAL SCHOOL.

3. This institution was founded to replace an Industrial School at Inchicore, which was the first establishment of the kind for boys certified in Ireland under the Industrial Schools Act. The Inchicore school was certified in May, 1869. It had, however, a very brief existence, for as it did not meet the requirements of the statute, the certificate was withdrawn in 1870. A committee of noblemen and gentlemen was then formed, and fifty-six acres of land, held in fee, were purchased at Artane, close to Dublin, with a view of establishing an efficient Industrial School. It

First Industrial School for Boys established at Inchicore.

Irish Christian Brothers.

was also decided to hand over its management to the Irish Christian Brothers. This confraternity was founded in 1802 by Edmund Ignatius Rice, with the aid and guidance of Dr. Hussey, Bishop of Waterford, the friend and correspondent of Burke. The Brotherhood follow a rule somewhat similar to that drawn up by the Abbé de la Salle of Reims, in the seventeenth century, and devote themselves to the work of education. In the autumn of 1831, the Government of Lord Grey determined to construct a thoroughly efficient system of primary education for the benefit of the people of Ireland. The views of the ministers were embodied in a very famous letter written by the late Lord Derby, then Mr. Stanley, and Chief Secretary to the Lord Lieutenant, which was published in the *Dublin Gazette* of December 8th, 1831. They were received with general satisfaction by the Catholics, and one of the most influential members of the hierarchy, Dr. Doyle, Bishop of Kildare and Leighlin, well known in controversial literature by his favourite signature, "J. K. L.", addressed a letter to his clergy in which he insisted that the proposals of the Government, although not perhaps the very best which could be devised, were well suited to the circumstances of the country. The Christian Brothers seem to have shared in the general enthusiasm, for they placed several of their schools under the newly constituted Board of National Education. Unfortunately, after a little time they considered the restrictions imposed on them by the new system would be fatal to the religious object of their Institute, and they eventually severed their connection with it. Their action in this respect is a matter of abiding regret. Experience has shown that there is nothing inherent in the National system to preclude religious orders from conscientiously helping to work it. But in the history of every idea there is a period of confusion when conceptions and misconceptions are in conflict. Moreover, it should be remembered, at the time the Christian Brothers withdrew from connection with the Board, there was a spirit abroad which made it most difficult or even impossible for the Commissioners to meet their wishes to any appreciable extent. Deep sympathies and broad views were essentially foreign to a generation saturated with the philosophy of Bentham, and whose leading men denounced Idealism with a virulence suggesting personal injury, as Porson said of the attack on Christianity by the historian of the Decline and Fall.

Certificate granted to Artane.

4. When the Industrial Schools Act was passed the Christian Brothers also showed some hesitation to undertake the management of schools certified under it. But the difficulties or misunderstandings were happily soon got over, and when the certificate was withdrawn from Inchicore, they agreed to take charge of the new school at Artane, selected Mr. Hoope as manager, and received their certificate on 9th July, 1870.

Opening of the School.

5. The boys were then transferred from Inchicore, and wooden huts were temporarily put up in the grounds at Artane pending the erection of permanent buildings. In 1870 96 boys were received there, but in the very next year the average number of

inmates rose to 233, and Mr. Hoope had already made successful arrangements for the instruction of boys in joinery, farm carpentering, machine and hand shoe making, tailoring, baking, smiths' work, and coopering.

6. In the year 1872 the average number of inmates was 336. In 1873 it rose to 433. Eleven additional acres of land were then acquired, and some new industries introduced into the school. In 1874 there was an average of 596 inmates, and in that year the Manager purchased forty-one adjoining acres of land. The present parade ground was then drained and asphalted. From this time the school has been steadily progressing, and at length has attained its present unique position amongst Industrial Schools. It has been visited by strangers from all parts of the world, and there is a universal consensus of opinion that it is nowhere surpassed. There are now 800 boys being trained within its walls. The buildings cover a superficial area of over two acres of land, and some £80,000 has been expended on them. In the workshops instruction is given in carpentering, engine-fitting, harness-making, painting, tailoring, weaving, hosiering, baking, &c.

Progress of the School.

7. The following table gives the number of boys who are receiving instruction in various trades:—

Bakery,	18	Painters,	9
Carpentering,	18	Smiths,	12
Farm Carpentering,	15	Shoemakers,	60
Cabinet Makers,	14	Tailors,	24
Harness Makers,	23	Weavers,	12
Engine Fitters and Wire Workers	22	Tinsmiths and Plumbers,	18
Plasterers,	8		

In all—253.

8. The next table shows what is taught in the schoolrooms:—

—	Reading.	Writing.	Arithmetic.	Grammar.	Geography.	Drawing South Kensington.
First Book,	58	58	58—Initiatory.	58—Initiatory.	58—Initiatory.	58
Second Book,	151	151	151	151—Initiatory.	151—Initiatory.	151
Third Book,	161	161	161	161	161	161
Fourth Book,	242	242	242	242	242	242
Fifth Book,	188	188	188	188	188	188
	800	800	800	800	800	800

9. The more advanced classes receive instruction in algebra, geometry, and shorthand.

10. From the time that Mr. Hoope undertook the management of this school very nearly 3,000 boys have passed through his hands. They are now settled in the world. Mr. Hoope can give the history of the vast majority of them, and he reports to me that almost all are doing well. It is not certainly too much to

say that were it not for the training of Artane, a very large proportion of these, instead of being as they are useful members of society, and a credit to their country, would now be men with lives blighted, perhaps many of them deprived of their liberty for crimes of various kinds, and bowed down by the weight of their own degradation, having as completely abandoned hope as the doomed spirits in Dante when they passed through the gate of the Inferno.

Successful results of Artane Training.

11. Besides the education, moral training, and discipline of Artane, one of the prime causes of its success was the practice of Mr. Hoope always to put boys, if possible, to trades to which respectable relatives belonged. He then took the greatest pains to make them efficient workmen, and in due course apprenticed them, if possible, to relatives. He found almost invariably that the relation of any boy was glad to receive him, or otherwise help to provide for him, and thus the lad was gradually restored to the position in life from which, by the death or misconduct of his parents, or other circumstances, he had fallen. The School of Artane is now firmly established, and its future is secure if those who govern it in time to come, while paying due attention to the wants of their own day, only adheres to the principles and traditions which shaped the conduct of its first manager.

Conditions of future success.

NUMBER OF SCHOOLS.

The following table shows the number of Reformatory and Industrial Schools existing in Ireland at the close of the year 1890 :—

—	REFORMATORIES SCHOOLS.		INDUSTRIAL SCHOOLS.	
	Roman Catholics.	Pro-testants.	Roman Catholics.	Pro-testants.
Number of Schools for Boys . . .	2	1	16	5
Do. Girls, . . .	3	1	42	6
Do. Young Boys and Girls,	-	-	1	-
Total, .	5	2	59	11

It will be perceived that there were 7 Reformatories and 70 Industrial Schools in active operation at the close of the year.

REFORMATORY SCHOOLS.

12. At the commencement of the year 1890 there were 8 Reformatory Schools in Ireland, containing 703 inmates. Three of these were Protestant establishments, and five were under Roman Catholic management. There were two Reformatory Schools for Protestant boys and one for girls; the Roman

Catholic Reformatories for boys were two in number, and for girls three. Owing to the persistant decrease in the number of committals, the Rehoboth-place Reformatory School in Dublin, which was founded in the year 1859 for Protestant boys, was closed last August. Hence, on the 31st of December last, there were seven Reformatory Schools, having under detention 744 persons, as against eight such schools, in which 763 inmates were detained, in the beginning of the year. Two of these are for Protestant children, one being situated in Dublin for girls, and the other in Belfast for boys. The three Roman Catholic Reformatory Schools for girls, viz., High Park Reformatory in Dublin, St. Joseph's in Limerick, and Spark's Lake, Monaghan, are all under the charge of the Nuns of the Good Shepherd. I can confirm the satisfactory reports of my predecessors as to their management, and Spark's Lake maintains its reputation for successful dealing with very refractory cases.

Closing of Rehoboth Reformatory School.

13. The two Roman Catholic schools for boys are at Philipstown, in the King's County, and at Glencree, in the Wicklow Hills. They are managed by the Oblate Fathers, a religious congregation which ought to be particularly well fitted to deal with criminals if it remains true to the spirit of its founder, Monseigneur de Mazenod, sometime Bishop of Marseilles, who died in 1861. Had this remarkable man lived before the "Divina Commedia" was adumbrated, he would surely have had his place in the "Paradiso," not indeed with Benedict or Bernard, but perhaps in the company of those two of whom we read in the eleventh canto:—

> L'un fu tutto serafico in ardore,
> L'altro per sapienza in terra fue,
> Di cherubica luce uno splendore.

His panegyric, however, has been composed by one of the greatest poets of our age, for the figure of Charles de Mazenod was present to the mind of Victor Hugo when he drew his famous picture of the ideal Christian bishop, and told how Monseigneur Myriel dealt with the crime and ingratitude, and touched the heart of the convict Valjean in the opening chapters of the *Misérables.*

The following table shows the number of persons who were discharged from each Reformatory School during the past year, and their subsequent behaviour:—

Discharges from Reformatory Schools.

[TABLE.

RETURN showing the Number of Children discharged from Reformatory Schools during the Year ending the 31st of December, 1890, and their subsequent characters;—.

—	Boys.				Girls.			
	Malone.	Rahoboth.	Philipstown.	Glencree.	Cork-street.	High Park.	St. Joseph's.	Spark's Lake.
MODE OF DISCHARGE—								
To employment,	8	2	22	30	1	2	1	5
Returned to friends,	10	7	11	23	-	-	3	4
Emigrated,	-	1	-	6	-	-	1	-
Sent to sea, or entered the Navy,	-	-	-	-	-	-	-	-
Enlisted,	2	-	4	4	-	-	-	-
Discharged on account of disease,	-	-	1	-	-	-	-	-
Discharged as incorrigible, or sentenced to penal servitude	1	1	-	-	-	-	-	-
Discharged as absconded,	-	-	-	-	-	-	-	-
Total,	21	11	38	66	1	2	5	9
SUBSEQUENT CHARACTER—								
Since died,	-	-	1	1	-	-	-	-
Doing well,	16	6	32	61	-	2	5	6
Doubtful,	-	2	-	-	-	-	-	2
Convicted of crime,	-	-	5	3	-	-	-	-
Unknown,	5	3	-	1	1	-	-	1
Recommitted to a Reformatory school	-	-	-	-	-	-	-	-
Total,	21	11	38	66	1	2	5	9

There were eight children transferred from one Reformatory to another; three from Rahoboth on its being closed. There were no girls transferred.

The above table tells the same satisfactory story as similar tables published in former reports, and as so much evidence may be found in them of the good results of the training in Reformatory schools, I do not propose to discuss the subject at any length on the present occasion. In connection, however, with the work expected from these schools, I cannot pass over a matter of supreme importance.

Sentences on Juvenile Criminals.

Juvenile criminals are sometimes committed to reformatories for so short a period that it is quite impossible for the Managers to do anything effective in the way of reforming them. All persons, without exception, who have considered the matter, and have practical experience, agree that sentences to a Reformatory should always be for the maximum limit of five years. This has been the invariable practice of the Police Magistrates of the city of Dublin. Unfortunately, the sentences passed in other courts are not so uniform. Country Magistrates, especially, seem often to forget that a five years sentence does not necessarily mean five years detention in a Reformatory School. They ignore the fact that Managers have power to license after half the sentence has expired, and may at any time obtain a discharge if they can show that it is for the advantage of the young offender. All the Managers, Protestant and Catholic, Oblates and Nuns of the Good Shepherd, complain that short sentences cripple their means of placing the young criminal at a distance from temptation, and in a way to earn a respectable livelihood. An illustration of short sentences is furnished by the history of Glencree. I have caused inquiry to be made into the career of every boy who has been admitted into the establishment since 1870, and I find that subsequent to discharge the percentages of re-convictions over the last 20 years are as follows:— Ill-effects of short sentences.

19 per cent.	of the boys committed for	5 years	were re-convicted.
16	"	"	4 "	"
19	"	"	3 "	"
28	"	"	2 "	"

and 40 per cent. of those who were discharged within a few months after admission found their way again into gaol. Other Reformatory schools could tell a similar tale, and such facts should induce Magistrates and Judges to pause before inflicting what they consider a merciful sentence on juvenile offenders.

Decrease of Juvenile Crime.

14. The subject of Reformatories leads naturally to the consideration of juvenile crime, and its steady decrease in Ireland is one of the most hopeful signs of the times in which we live.

15. The following tables will show the sentences passed on juveniles in Ireland in the years 1870 and 1890. It will be seen that the number of children convicted of crime has decreased by over 50 per cent. in the year 1890 as compared with 20 years before.

[Table.

SENTENCES PASSED ON JUVENILES IN 1870 AND 1890.

For Year 1870.

Terms of Sentence.	Age. Under 10 Years. M.	Age. Under 10 Years. F.	Age. 10 Years and not exceeding 16. M.	Age. 10 Years and not exceeding 16. F.	Total. M.	Total. F.
Penal Servitude—						
For 5 Years,	-	-	1	-	1	-
Imprisonment—						
12 Months,	-	-	3	-	[illegible]	-
6 Months,	-	-	7	-	7	-
3 and 2 Months,	-	-	66	11	66	11
1 Month,	4	1	166	80	170	[illegible]
Short Periods,	93	-	600	107	[illegible]	107
	97	1	842	138	[illegible]	[illegible]

For Year 1890.

Terms of Sentence.	Age. Under 10 Years. M.	Age. Under 10 Years. F.	Age. 10 Years and not exceeding 16. M.	Age. 10 Years and not exceeding 16. F.	Total. M.	Total. F.
Penal Servitude—						
For 5 Years,	-	-	-	-	-	-
Imprisonment—						
12 Months,	-	-	-	-	-	-
6 Months,	-	-	1	1	1	1
3 and 2 Months,	6	-	29	2	35	2
1 Month,	4	2	85	8	89	10
Short Periods,	17	7	[illegible]	51	616	[illegible]
	24	9	857	63	881	71

The following Table will show the number of children in Reformatory Schools on 31st of December of each of the following years.

—	Boys.	Girls.	Total.
1880, ...	[illegible]	232	1,160
1881, ...	936	[illegible]	1,148
1882, ...	[illegible]	184	1,140
1883, ...	907	189	[illegible]
1884, ...	875	175	1,063
1885, .	814	153	[illegible]
1886, ...	791	145	[illegible]
1887, ...	726	133	[illegible]
1888, ...	749	118	855
1889, ...	646	115	763
1890, ...	628	116	744

16. During this period three Reformatory Schools have been closed, and it will be seen there has been a persistent decrease of juvenile convictions from year to year, and that the number has fallen from 1,160 in 1880 to 744 in 1890, which is a fall of over 35 per cent.

17. This diminution of juvenile crime cannot be accounted for altogether by the decrease of population. It is largely owing, in my opinion, to the work of the Reformatories. They have been the means of breaking up the societies of little pickpockets and burglars apprentices in our cities and towns; and, as a result, the hardened young scoundrel who flourished half a century ago, and whose mode of action is so familiar to the readers of *Oliver Twist*, has become a rare specimen of humanity. In considering, however, the causes of the persistent annual decrease of juvenile crime, the action of the Industrial Schools must be taken chiefly into account. They were instituted for the purpose of rescuing the street arab and other vagrant children from the snares of the tempter, and they have done their work so efficiently as to become now almost substitutes for Reformatories.

Industrial Schools.

18. The first Industrial School in the United Kingdom was founded in Aberdeen exactly fifty years since. This was, however, merely a day-school, and children were not under legal restraint. In 1854, an Act was passed for Scotland under which certain children could be sent to an Industrial School. The main provisions of this legislation were extended to England some three years later. Ireland owes her schools to an Act passed in the year 1868, when the late Lord Mayo was Chief Secretary to the Lord Lieutenant.

First Industrial School in United Kingdom.

The Irish Industrial Schools Act.

General disregard of Practical Education previous to passing of Industrial Schools Act.

19. Previous to the passing of this Act, there was a general disregard of practical education. The young men of the country the sons of small farmers and shopkeepers, in consequence of their early years having been spent in purely literary work, or in endeavouring to master the higher branches of arithmetic and mathematics, strove to escape from their fathers' business and from all industrial pursuits. The girls of the same class were also educated as if they were all to be engaged exclusively in intellectual occupations. They did not know how to perform ordinary household duties. They knew nothing of such important matters as elementary cookery, were not handy with their needle, and earned for themselves a general character for untidiness. The National Board is not to blame for this, seeing that it has made constant efforts to foster Industrial Training. It was the result of erroneous views on education held almost universally fifty years since, and which, unfortunately, prevail largely still. The working of the Industrial Schools Act has done much to modify public opinion.

Object of Industrial School.

But as Industrial Schools were established for the purpose of rescuing children who were in danger of falling into the criminal classes, only a limited section of the population has been able to profit by them. Nevertheless, the great practical good they have accomplished has made a deep impression on the mind of the country.

20. Since their establishment up to 31st December last 19,073 children, 8,867 being boys and 10,206 girls, have been trained in them, and the vast majority of these children have been a marked success in life.

21. There are 50 Roman Catholic Schools and 11 Protestant. All the former have their full complement.

Protestant Industrial Schools.

22. As regards the 11 Protestant Schools, some of them are very much below their certified number. This is especially the case in Cork, where there are two Schools for Protestant boys, namely, St. Nicholas' and the Boys' Home, Marble Hill. Both of these Institutions are in a most unsatisfactory condition; neither of them has over reached its limit, and both have, for a considerable number of years, been much below it. I am decidedly of opinion these two Schools should be amalgamated, and in this view my predecessor, Dr. Plunkett O'Farrell, heartily concurs. It would be then possible for the Protestants of Cork to establish a really good Male Industrial School; which might, perhaps, in time compete in excellence even with the Meath School for Protestant boys at Blackrock, Dublin.

23. The following table shows the numbers of inmates in the Industrial Schools at the close of 1889 and 1890, showing the religion and sex :—

—	1889.			1890.		
	Boys.	Girls.	Total.	Boys.	Girls.	Total.
Roman Catholics, ...	2,667	4,042	6,709	2,991	4,131	[illegible]
Protestants, ...	582	283	865	368	277	[illegible]
	3,249	4,325	7,574	3,359	4,408	7,767

DISCHARGES.

24. During the past year 1,342 children were discharged, transferred from, or died in, Industrial Schools, 645 being boys, and 697 girls, and the following table shows how they were disposed of:—

—	Boys.	Girls.	Total.
To employment or service,	318	398	716
Returned to Friends,	126	180	306
Emigrated,	27	46	73
Sent to Sea,	8	—	8
Enlisted,	6	—	6
Specially discharged,	16	3	19
Committed to Reformatories,	7	1	8
Transferred,	101	3	104
Died,	37	65	[illegible]
Absconders discharged by expiration of sentence,	5	1	6
Discharged on account of insufficient grounds of detention,	6	10	16
	645	697	1,342

25. It will be observed that 318 boys and 398 girls were put to employment or service, making a total of 716. Last year 616 were so placed; the same number exactly went to sea and enlisted in both years. The total number who emigrated in 1889 was 67, and the number in 1890 was 73. But as the total discharges in 1890 exceeded those in 1889 by 120, it will be observed that the percentage of emigrants upon the whole number of discharges has considerably decreased.

26. I am glad to be able to state that the number of committals on insufficient grounds have diminished during the past year; at the same time they occur much too frequently. The grounds of committal under the Industrial Schools Act (Ireland), 1868 (31 Vic., cap. 25), are clearly set forth in the circular sent to Magistrates from time to time since the year 1873. Informal committals.

Notwithstanding this, many mistakes are made, and it becomes my duty so often to return the Committal Order for amendment, that, in my opinion, as was suggested by the Royal Commission of 1882, one of the two Justices who must sign the Order, should, if possible, be a Resident Magistrate, and the Order itself should only be made upon evidence taken in open court and after a remand and inquiry by the police.

[TABLE.

FINANCIAL STATEMENT—REFORMATORY SCHOOLS.

Financial Statement Reformatory Schools.

The following table shows the amount received for Reformatory Schools during the two past years :—

—	1889.			1890.			Increase.			Decrease.		
	£	s.	d.	£	s.	d.	£	s.	d.	£	s.	d.
Received from Treasury,	12,716	7	10	11,890	6	1	—			826	1	9
Do. Local Rates, .	5,986	5	1	5,518	16	11	—			467	8	2
Do. other sources,	518	9	8	430	0	2	—			88	9	6
Estimated profits, . .	1,000	0	0	987	7	8½	—			12	12	3½
Total, . .	20,217	0	7	18,886	10	4½	—			1,330	10	2½

It will be seen that there has been a considerable decrease, amounting to £1,300 10s. 2½d., in the receipts during the past year over that for 1889. As regards the amount received from the Treasury there has been a saving of £826 1s. 9d.

The total amount expended during the past year was £17,100 8s. 7d., which was laid out under the following sixteen items:—

	£	s.	d.		£	s.	d.
				Brought forward,	14,030	5	4
Salaries of Officers, . .	8,069	15	0	Travelling, &c., . .	303	15	3
Rations for do., . .	1,306	14	4	Medical Expenses, . .	261	4	10
Food for Inmates, . .	6,431	15	11	Sundries, Rewards, &c., .	587	2	5
Clothing for do., . .	1,676	14	7	Rent, ...	329	5	7
Washing, Fuel, Light, .	1,229	11	10	Interest, . . .	169	19	1
Repairs, Rates and Taxes, .	940	0	11	Disposal, . . .	498	1	1
Furniture and Sundries, .	506	17	7	Building, . . .	178	1	8
Printing, &c., . . .	239	18	3	Loss on Industrial Department, . . .	—		
	£14,030	5	4		£17,100	8	7

The expenditure for 1889 amounted to £19,401 5s. 11d. It will therefore be seen that there was a decrease of £2,210 17s. 2d.

The following table shows the actual cost of each child in each Reformatory School in Ireland during the past year:—

Boys.	£	s.	d.	Girls.	£	s.	d.
Malone, ...	31	9	9	Cork-street, . . .	22	10	6
Rehoboth-place, . . .	31	6	0	High Park, . . .	18	8	6
Philipstown, . . .	18	13	3	St. Joseph's Limerick, . .	21	8	4
Glencree, ...	22	15	1	Spark's Lake, . . .	23	8	11

It will be observed that the average cost for each child was £22 19s. 8d. In 1889 it was £22 12s. 7d.

This return bears very favourably with those of previous years, and while every care is taken to keep down the expenditure a due regard is observed in maintaining these schools in their present creditable condition.

Financial Statement—Industrial Schools.

During the past year the amount received for the support and maintenance of children in Industrial Schools came to £158,184 16s. 2d. The following Table shows the amounts received during the past two years under the various sources of revenue.

Financial Statement Industrial Schools.

—	1889.			1890.			Increase.			Decrease.		
	£	s.	d.	£	s.	d.	£	s.	d.	£	s.	d.
Received from Treasury,	93,506	15	5	95,842	1	9	2,335	6	5		—	
Do. Local Rates,	34,558	14	1	37,262	3	0½	2,709	7	11½		—	
Do. Other Sources,	6,[illegible]	16	7	7,[illegible]	0	0	1,[illegible]7	3	1		—	
Estimated Profits,	10,000	0	0	12,075	15	7	2,075	15	7		—	
Total,	144,697	8	1	158,183	3	11½	8,448	17	10½		—	

I am glad to point out that there has been a large income derived from industrial profits of over £12,000, which is an increase of about £2,000 over the previous year. This sum is made up largely by farm and garden produce, and such industries as carpentry, tailoring, shoemaking, washing, knitting, weaving, &c. The larger portion of produce grown, and of work done is for the benefit of the schools, and the local markets were not affected to any appreciable extent by what was sold.

The expenditure amounted to £158,274 1s. 1d., as shown in the following table:—

	£	s.	d.		£	s.	d.
Salaries of Officers,	14,157	19	7	Medical Expenses,	2,407	14	6
Rations for do.,	8,678	19	0	Sundries, Rewards,	2,370	2	6½
Food for Inmates,	60,528	1	2½	Rent,	3,684	14	5
Clothing for do.,	20,256	1	5	Interest,	3,371	3	4
Washing, Fuel, Light,	11,511	6	3½	Disposal,	3,277	13	0
Repairs, Rates, and Taxes,	6,378	16	9½	Building,	6,581	10	1
Furniture and Sundries,	6,477	17	8½	Loss on Industrial Department,	80	4	5
Printing, &c.,	5,070	7	6				
Travelling,	768	3	6½	Total,	158,274	1	1

In the year before it amounted to £156,789 14s. 9d., thus showing an increase of £1,484 6s. 4d.

The cost for each child during the past year averaged £17 13s.

The total amount collected for parental money is herewith given:—

—	Reformatories	Industrial Schools	Total
	£ s. d.	£ s. d.	£ s. d.
Dublin, . .	208 4 9	148 9 3	356 14 0
Provinces, .	167 9 8	409 12 8	577 2 4
Total, . . .	375 14 5	558 1 11	920 16 4

In 1889, the total amount collected came to £901 16s. 9d., so that there has been an increase of £20 19s. 7d.

I have caused two new tables to be added to the Appendices showing the number of children under detention in Reformatory and Industrial Schools belonging to the different counties and towns in Ireland on the 31st of last December, also those who were admitted from each county and town during the year. The sum contributed from each county and town for their support will be found in the Appendices.

Education.

General principles of education.

27. The subject of Education in Reformatory and Industrial Schools should of course be conducted on the same principles as guide the general education of the country. The main object of all school training is to teach people to think. It cannot be said that a child is being properly educated who merely learns formulæ by heart, or to repeat answers to difficult questions without the slightest notion of their meaning. To train the minds of children there is nothing better than to let them deal with a subject with which they are conversant. An excellent illustration of this was given by the late Dr. W. K. Sullivan in his evidence before the Select Committee on Irish Industries in 1885. He states that some years previously he had to visit some of the primary schools of the country and report upon them, when he was a member of the Royal Commission of Inquiry into Primary Education. On one occasion he gave the children first a passage from Cardinal Newman, and then an extract from a book dealing with peat bog. The literary passage was completely lost upon them, but they understood perfectly the extract upon the subject of the bog, although it was full of technical terms, botanical expressions, and hard names, because the object itself was all around, and it was a matter with which they were perfectly familiar. Only within the last few days I have myself gone through an experience very similar to that of Dr. Sullivan.

Three essential subjects of education. Reading.

28. The three essential subjects of primary education are, of course, reading, writing, and arithmetic. Of these reading, as far as boys' schools are concerned, seems to me the most unsatisfactory. To read with correct taste and true expression is so rare, even under conditions implying a far higher degree of intellectual

culture than can be expected from children in industrial schools, that we have no right to expect it from them. But it is not too much to require that any intelligent child should pay some sort of attention to the subject-matter about which he reads. This is not always done. Boys when asked to explain what they had been reading about, sometimes gave the most ludicrous answers, plainly showing their teachers very rarely put them through this intellectual exercise. A fair proficiency has commonly been attained in writing, and the copy-books in use prove that teachers generally understand what an excellent discipline it is for a boy to be obliged to keep his copy-book neat and clean. I am not sure, however, that too much importance may not sometimes be attached to the penmanship in copy-books as compared with writing from dictation. Still I am bound to add, that in a general way the spelling of ordinary words is well taught. The attainments in arithmetic seem to me to be exceedingly satisfactory.

Writing.

Arithmetic.

29. Speaking generally, then, as regards these Reformatory and Industrial Schools, I am disposed to think that, from a literary point of view, the education given in them is quite high enough. If it errs at all, perhaps it is in aiming at too much. At Artane, for instance, the more advanced classes are, as I have already stated, taught algebra, geometry, and shorthand, and many of the boys have reached a certain proficiency in those branches of study. This is the principal school under this department which is not inspected by an official of the National Board. But I venture to say that, taking all things into consideration, it will compare fairly with almost any school of primary education in the kingdom. I am glad to be able to report equally favourably of the great majority of the other schools. Not, however, of all. A few were unsatisfactory, and especially one situated in a southern county.

Education generally satisfactory.

30. In this school there were boys of fourteen, fifteen, and sixteen years of age, who after spending many years in the institution were presented for examination in the third and fourth class. This was in itself disgraceful, and was rendered more so by the fact that these boys failed badly even in such a low class. The arithmetic was particularly bad, and in the junior classes, although several boys brought out the answers to their sums correctly, they all reckoned on their fingers. Work done in this manner is almost entirely worthless, and indicates a wretched method of instruction. Of course it would be impossible for me to avoid making a special report on this school with a view of a withdrawal of the certificate, unless I had reason to hope that very considerable changes are likely to be made, and drastic and far-reaching measures of reform soon carried out.

Some exceptions.

31. There is one great deficiency in the boys' Industrial schools of Ireland, and that is the almost total absence of instruction in agriculture. Nevertheless, agricultural education is a matter of life and death to Ireland. Farming is the chief occupation of the

Agriculture.

people and must remain so, although the economical production of such gases as hydrogen and oxide of carbon must increase the importance of the gas engine, and possibly result in numerous small workshops being established able to compete with great factories. Moreover, it is an industry which can derive immense benefits from the teaching of science. The farmers of the country have now obtained a substantial interest in their land, but they can only realize a very small part of the fruit of recent legislation without the highest knowledge and skill. It is idle for the Irish agriculturist to look forward to Protection to save him from the competition of North America, to which will soon be added that of two other continents. His only chance is to learn his business, not only practically but theoretically, to advance, and not look back, and to substitute a system more like kitchen-garden culture for the present rude tillage, which only embraces the cultivation of three or four plants. A certain percentage of these boys are certain to become in one form or another agriculturists, yet they have not the slightest idea how to carry on such industry. His Excellency the Lord Lieutenant, during his recent visit to the south of Ireland, pointed out that Kerry, for instance, could produce spring vegetables at least a fortnight earlier than most English Shires, and he insisted on the facility which the opening up of the county by Light Railways would give vegetable growers to send their produce to the great markets of the kingdom. If they are to do this, some special training will be necessary.

School at Upton specially suited for an agricultural school.

32. In connection with this subject I cannot but think that it would be most advisable for at least one of the boys' industrial schools to be devoted mainly to the training of agriculturalists. The school at Upton would be specially suited for such work; the buildings are large and commodious, having cost about £20,000 to erect them; the situation is admirable; there is a very large farm attached to the institution. The railway communication is such as to afford great facilities for the transaction of business at fairs and markets; the distance from Cork is not great, and a model agricultural school could be established in which practical education in agriculture could be carried on to the highest extent without infringing on the supposed rights of workmen, and without even the suspicion of competing unfairly with any existing trade.

Ackerbau Schulen, Germany.

33. It should be formed mainly on the lines of the "Ackerbau Schulen," of Germany. These schools impart to country lads high practical skill in agriculture, particularly in the use of improved implements and agricultural machines; and endeavour to make them fit to manage small farms, to act as foremen, to make and mend implements, &c. About one-third of the scholar's time in such a school is devoted to theoretical subjects, and about two-thirds to practical working on the land, in the workshop, or in the farm offices. In the kingdom of Prussia there are as many as 32 of these schools for farming; in the kingdom of Würtemberg there are 4; in Bavaria there are 8; and very many

more are scattered about the States of the empire. Similar institutions exist in France, and some of them are specially deserving of notice, particularly one known as La Pilletière, in Sarthe, to which is attached a farm as nearly as possible of the same size as that at Upton, and very similar as regards the quality of the land. The good done by these agricultural schools, especially in Germany, is hard to over-estimate. They are undoubtedly one of the main causes why the Germans are so successful as emigrants, and why the German race has established itself so firmly in America, and must surely in time to come exercise a commanding influence in shaping the destinies of the United States. The first agricultural school in Germany was established in Prussia by the father of Frederick the Great, at Königshorst, in Brandenburg, about 170 years ago. It is another instance of the solid work done by that extraordinary man, who fills such a striking place in Prussian history between his noble and heroic grandfather, the Great Elector, and his brilliant and unconquerable son. Doctor Berghaus, in his *Landbuch der Mark Brandenburg*, published in 1854, gives an account of the great results produced by this school, especially in butter-making. It was the first institution of its kind founded in Europe. The first agricultural school was not established in France till some forty years afterwards. It was founded at Rochette, near Melun, in the last years of the reign of Louis XV.

First agricultural school in Germany founded.

First agricultural school in France.

34. This also produced great results in France; but it is not necessary to go to past history or to foreign countries to understand the importance of an agricultural school. The effect of the excellent training given in the Munster Dairy School is already beginning to affect the whole system of butter-making in Ireland. Girls taught there are now spreading the improved system in Ulster and Connaught. If a school were established for boys at Upton, in which lads could be taught thoroughly the knowledge of different kinds of soil, their reclamation and cultivation, the manufacture and repairing of implements and machines, the laying out of manure pits, the knowledge of seeds, the carrying out of simple farm accounts, the breeding of horses, cattle, sheep, and pigs; the methods of rearing the calf, the quantity and quality of milk which should be given it, the cultivation of fruit, and, in short, all matters pertaining to the calling of an agriculturalist, an effect could not fail to be produced throughout the province of Munster which would in a quarter of a century change the face of every county in it.

Effect of Munster Dairy School.

35. As regards the schools under Nuns, the immense majority of them are in a thoroughly efficient state, and the Girls' Schools for Protestants are also on the whole satisfactory. With respect to the three subjects of reading, writing, and arithmetic, I should say the average reading of girls is somewhat superior to that of boys; and as for fulfilling the object for which Industrial Schools were instituted, the records of female schools are perhaps rather better than those of male. I find, for instance, that 382 girls have within the last

Female schools.

twenty years left the school managed by the Nuns of the Good Shepherd, Sunday's Well, Cork. Of these 368 have done well, six have been lost sight of, and only eight are known to have turned out badly. Other institutions show similar records.

Loughrea Dairy School.

I am glad to observe considerable activity in the way of introducing new industries into the female schools. The Manager of Loughrea School, for instance, some year or so ago, established a Dairy Farm. It has been a success. A competent person trained in the Munster Dairy School has been engaged by the Nuns to instruct the children, and there is every reason to hope that good results will follow.

Farm for rearing poultry, Newtownforbes.

36. A more remarkable attempt to introduce a special industry into the country has been made at Newtownforbes. The Manager of this school established, in the month of April, 1890, a Farm for rearing Poultry on a considerable scale. Poultry houses and suitable appliances and the best breeds were obtained. Notwithstanding some failures, which were to be expected at starting, the school has succeeded in bringing to perfection Brown Leghorns, Black Minorcas, Houdans, Orpingtons, Light Brahams, Buff Cochins, Black Hamburgs, Cockerels, &c. The Manager deserves great credit for this most meritorious attempt to introduce into the country an improved method of rearing poultry. There can be no doubt that, if this industry were to spread and commend itself to the people, it would do much to promote the comfort of our agricultural population.

Instruction in poultry farming given in France.

In view of the importance of poultry to small farmers and labourers, the French Government founded the École Pratique d'Aviculture. It was established on the 27th of February, 1888, at Gambais, in the Department of the Seine et Oise, with the object of showing the rural population how poultry should be bred and reared. There are no expensive appliances. Hundreds of chickens are hatched artificially, and the methods employed to feed them are such that they become fit for the table at four months old. This experiment is now attracting the attention of several European Governments, notably that of Prussia, and of some of the other Governments of the various Confederated States linked together by the Imperial Crown of Germany. The birds sold at Gambais realize a net profit of about one shilling and sixpence a head. In Ireland the profit would be larger, for our food supply is cheaper; and it is certain that if our small agricultural holders were only taught the proper way of rearing, dressing, and sending their poultry to market, they would add very considerably indeed to their income.

Weaving, St. Coleman's, Queenstown.

37. I wish also to call attention to another industry which was started in the month of October last. Two members of the community of St. Coleman's Convent of Mercy, Queenstown, went for a month to Skibbereen, in order to study the weaving industry which is established there. On their return, looms were erected and a weaving school built at a considerable cost. The girls are now taught by a skilled instructor, whose time is divided between Skibbereen and Queenstown. It is too

soon to offer any opinion as to the future of this industry. Undoubtedly the quality of work done is excellent, and should it prove a success, it will not only be a great benefit to the school, but will also give employment to the children of needy and destitute parents in the neighbourhood.

38. It must, however, be borne in mind that weaving has already been tried in several of the Industrial Schools in Ireland without profitable results other than those gained by the pupils in acquiring mechanical knowledge and skill. If factories or mills were in existence as in England or the North of Ireland, where children who were taught weaving could find employment, they would, of course, receive direct benefit; but it is very doubtful whether hand-made cotton or woollen goods will ever be able to compete in price with manufactured articles in the open market.

Lace-making.

39. In many of the schools lacemaking is taught. This is no doubt a desirable industry for grown girls who have a real taste for it, especially in such localities as Killarney, much frequented by tourists, where there is a great demand for lace in the summer. I do not think, however, that it is a suitable industry, generally speaking, for children in industrial schools. These children have so many things to acquire, that they cannot give the time and attention necessary to make fine Irish point lace, and it should never be forgotten that inferior lace made by hand is quite valueless, in consequence of the large quantities of the article manufactured by machinery throughout Europe. Household duties are what girls in an Industrial School ought to learn. Knitting, plain sewing, making and mending various articles of clothing, and a knowledge of cooking would be much more useful to them than lacemaking, and would make them useful servants, of which there is such a dearth in the country.

Prime importance of household duties being taught.

40. While on this subject I would urge the managers of female schools to consider the possibility of having rooms furnished with all the appliances necessary for domestic usage, in which girls could be trained to discharge effectively the duties of servants. Ordinary school-rooms with the usual fittings are useless for this purpose. Girls should be accustomed to handle glass and china; taught to polish and keep clean highly finished steel grates and fire irons, to take up and clean carpets, to fold curtains and linen, and to perform all duties connected with the kitchen, still-room, and pantry. They would, if so trained, be sure of occupation immediately on leaving school; while girls who come out having passed successful examinations in the usual books, with even perhaps a smattering of French, and who are experts in lacemaking, weaving, card painting, piano playing, may be exposed, while in search of employment, to all the dangers and temptations inseparable from want.

41. The convent schools of this country are such models of cleanliness and order that, if managers would only make a serious effort in the direction I suggest, they would double the usefulness of the female industrial schools of Ireland.

"SPECIAL CLASS OF INDUSTRIAL SCHOOLS."

Baltimore Fishing School.

42. Some Industrial Schools have been established for special purposes. The Piscatorial School at Baltimore, Co. Cork, was founded to teach boys fishing, curing of fish, net-making, and all things pertaining to a fisherman's calling. The little village of Baltimore is situated in the south-west corner of Ireland, in sight of Cape Clear. In the early part of the 17th century there was already a fair fishing industry round that coast, but during the Civil Wars, like most other branches of Irish trade, it was almost annihilated.

Irish Fishing Industry.

Nevertheless it seems strange that the Irish Fishing Industry should be in its present backward state, for Ireland possesses a coast which, taking into account the indentation of bays and estuaries, is over two thousand three hundred miles in length, so that few countries can command such an extent of ocean and shore. It is commonly said in explanation that the sea has no attraction for so-called Celts. This is one of those conventional views so welcome to the vulgar, seeing that it enables them to arrive at what seems a satisfactory conclusion without much knowledge or thought. It bears a strong likeness to the theories about the ten lost tribes of Israel which are sometimes even still put forward to solve ethnological difficulties, and is equally unsupported by the evidence of history. The Celts were a people belonging to the southern European branch of the Aryan race. They formerly inhabited the Alpine countries and South Germany, then drove back the Basques in France to the west and south, and crossed to the British Islands. It so happens that those of them who came to Ireland were the heroes of the legendary voyages said to have been undertaken in the twilight times of Irish history, which made a deep impression on the mind of Europe in the middle ages, and incited the mariners of the fifteenth century to set out on their perilous wanderings in quest of the secrets of the ocean. But the stories told of the mythical adventures of St. Brendan and other similar tales could only have sprung from the imagination of a people who knew and loved the sea. The population of Britanny is Celtic, and readers of French naval history do not require to be reminded of its sea-faring capacity. The name of Cape Breton, the Islands of St. Pierre and Miquelon, the discovery of the estuary of the St. Lawrence by Jacques Cartier, the traditions of the town of St. Malo, not to mention the history of Newfoundland and the Peace of Utrecht, recall facts totally inconsistent with the assertion that there is something in the constitution of the Celt which unfits him to be a sailor. Hardihood, daring, presence of mind and activity, are the prime qualifications for a seaman, and those who know the West Coast of Ireland, and have seen how men in skiffs made of canvas and hoops will face in wild weather the waves of the Atlantic, can judge whether Irishmen are deficient in these qualifications.

The cause of the backward state of Irish fisheries must be sought elsewhere. It is due to the policy which so long prevailed as regards all Irish industries, the story of which has been so succinctly told by Lord Dufferin in his excellent little volume on Irish emigration and the tenure of land in Ireland. To go into this matter would be too much of a digression from my special task. Suffice it to say, that in the year 1810 the Irish fishing industry had almost ceased to exist. In that year a new Fishery Board was appointed. The duties of this Board, which came to an end in 1830, were to construct and improve fishery harbours, and to grant bounties on the tonnage, cure, capture, and export of fish. The effect of its operations was marvellous. In the year 1821 the number of vessels engaged in fishing was 4,489, and the number of men and boys who were partially or wholly employed in fishing was 21,441. When the Board's operations ceased in 1830, there were 13,110 vessels engaged in sea fishing, and the number of men and boys wholly or partially employed in them was 64,741. As has been the case with many institutions in Ireland, just as its operations began to bear fruit, its actions were paralysed and its existence came to an end. In the year 1844 the Irish Reproductive Loan Society of London offered a sum of £5,000 to the Board of Works as loans to fishermen. The Board did not consider itself at liberty to administer the gift. In 1846 they accepted an equal sum for erecting curing houses. Seven of these were built, and they not only provided a market for fishermen, but furnished technical workshops for the fishing population. Just at the moment when they promised to be most useful they were closed. This was in the disastrous year of 1848, when it would have been easy to create a fishing industry which in a short time would have required no help, and when a great nursery for fishermen existed in the population of the coast.

In 1848 however Adam Smith still reigned supreme in the domain of economic science. In England no one challenged his fundamental ideas. But in that very year Bruno Hildebrand published his well-known book, *Die Nationaleconomie der Gegenwart und Zukunft.* It dealt a deadly blow to the rationalistic method then in the ascendant. Karl Kniess followed, and after him Brentano, Held, Schmoller, Nasse, Schæffle, Rösler, Adolf Wagner, and a host of others, who applied to the economic system the method adopted by Savigny in the domain of jurisprudence and created the German historical school of political economy. The leading idea of this school is to accentuate the moral element in economic science, and it learnt from Hegel the great truth that the State is an ethical organism and not merely an institution for the preservation of order. This enunciation has now been carried forward into the public throng of men, and in every country it has altered the notions hitherto common as to the functions, constitution, and nature of the State. The State is now looked upon as the organ of the nation for all ends which cannot be effected by voluntary effort. This idea has got firm possession of the mind of Europe and the result may be observed in the tendency of recent legislation both at home and abroad. It manifests itself among other ways in the changed attitude of opinion as to the wisdom of public authority assisting and supervising efforts to develop the industrial resources of Ireland, and it finds expression in such institutions as Baltimore school.

Establishment of Baltimore. Almost immediately after the passing of the Industrial Schools Act, it was urged that a school should be established somewhere in the South of Ireland, in which boys should be taught seamanship and the curing of fish. Kinsale would have been the natural place to have established such an institution, for the inhabitants of the district have always been considered as the best seamen on the southern coast, and the place had railway communication with the City of Cork. Nothing, however, was done at Kinsale, and so things remained till the Rev. Charles Davis was appointed parish priest at Baltimore. He set his heart on establishing a Piscatory School in this village; and mainly through his untiring energy the present institution has come into existence.

He was munificently assisted by His Grace the Duke of Norfolk, Baroness Burdett Coutts, Lord Iveagh, and others. Boats of a sufficient size and build for Atlantic fishing were procured, suitable buildings erected, a free grant of £5,000 given by the present Government, and towards the close of the year I was able to certify that accommodation existed for 150 boys, the number it at present contains.

Education and Training. 43. These boys are taught to make and mend nets, to handle fish and manage boats. Their elementary education is also not neglected, and the result of a recent examination held by the Science and Art Department shows adequate instruction is given in the principles of navigation. The Rev. Mr. Green, one of the Inspectors of Irish Fisheries, in his recent inspection of the coast, had on board his ship two Baltimore boys. He met with very tempestuous weather, and the seamanship of his crew was thoroughly tested. He informs me that he was much struck by the conduct of these lads, and that one of them especially behaved in a manner which would have done credit to any sailor in Her Majesty's navy. It is, however, to be regretted that more efficient steps are not taken to start such boys fairly in life after they leave the school. Mr. Green also tells me he found seven splendid lads recently discharged from Baltimore breaking stones in Arran. While on this subject, I cannot refrain from saying that special legislation for schools like Baltimore seems necessary. Whatever may be said as to the advisability of discharging children from Industrial Schools at the age of sixteen, it seems clear for instance that no such obligation should exist in the case of this Piscatorial School. This will be evident if we bear in mind that it is not possible to expose boys to the fatigue and hardship of a fishing expedition in the Atlantic before they reach the age of fourteen years. Hence, if they are discharged at sixteen, they have only two years experience of the boats—much too short a time for an average boy of that class to learn his calling. Moreover, I think some arrangements should be made to prevent boys who have no connexion with the sea being

Special legislation seems necessary.

committed to this Institution. As the law now stands, there is nothing to prevent any boy who is found begging, or wandering and without proper guardianship, from being sent there, no matter whether he is physically fit to be a fisherman or not, or has any special aptitude for the calling. The conception of a Fishing School is a new departure in the industrial school system, and the institution may fairly claim exceptional consideration. On the other hand, it should be managed with exceptional care, if it is to fulfil the end for which it has been called into existence. The usefulness of such an establishment must be measured by the success in life of the boys trained in it. But this must be very problematical unless particular care is taken to give them a fair start in the world. All industrial schools efficiently managed pay special attention to this point. The managers of the Meath School for Protestant boys at Blackrock have an admirable system for the purpose. The Christian Brothers at Artane follow a similar method. In Roman Catholic schools, managed by other religious orders, there is usually one member of the community told off to supervise boys on licence preparatory to discharge, and to watch their progress for at least three years after they have been fully emancipated from controul. If this paramount duty is to be efficiently performed at Baltimore, the Committee of Management will have, I think, to consider whether, in view of the various important and pressing calls on the time of the Rev. Mr. Davis, he should not be provided with an increased staff. I have also to observe, with considerable regret, that three branches of industry essential to a fisherman's calling are not taught at Baltimore. The boys receive no instruction in boat-building, carpentering, or cooperage. Considering, however, what has been achieved already, and the zeal of those who are responsible for the school, I cannot but hope that in the near future they will see their way to remedy these grave deficiencies.

Necessity of a system for starting boys fairly in life.

"Nuns Schools for Junior Boys."

44. There is another special class of schools to which I beg to call attention, namely, Nuns' schools for junior boys. These are, generally speaking, admirable institutions. They are the means of rescuing boys from the temptation of the streets at a very early age and impressing upon their tender minds sound moral doctrines. Of these junior schools, Passage West, Cork, which is under the care of Sisters of Mercy, especially deserves notice. I heartily agree with what has been said in its praise by my predecessors. It would be difficult or impossible to point out anything defective in its management. The boys, when they have to leave it, are particularly well qualified to profit by any instruction they may receive, owing to the special attention paid to their physical as well as their moral training.

Passage West School.

45. Managers of senior schools have repeatedly told me they were always glad to get Passage West boys, for they found them remarkable for their truthfulness and cheerful open manner, the result, no doubt, of the teaching of the nuns and of the happy childhood which they passed under the care of those excellent ladies.

GENERAL OBSERVATIONS.

Buildings.

46. I am happy to say that the buildings are, as a rule, in a very fair condition, and judging by the reports of former years there is a distinct improvement in their general character. A few of the Institutions are, however, still without proper buildings, but in some of these alterations are being made which will make them more suited for the purposes of an Industrial School.

Corporal Punishment.

47. Although I have to complain that in the majority of the schools the punishment book is very inadequately kept, and frivolous and incredible excuses have been offered for the delinquencies of managers in this respect, still I have every reason to believe that very little punishment is required, and that corporal chastisement is rarely inflicted. It has, however, sometimes to be resorted to, and in this case the person who sees the offence should not be allowed to administer the punishment. No boy should be struck with the hand on any consideration. The cane, I also think, should not be used; its application is dangerous to such children as are in Industrial Schools, even when not applied on the hand. The wale frequently suppurating in subjects where the vital energies are below par may sometimes cause grave mischief, and injudicious corporal chastisement provokes sentimental people to call out against this mode of punishment altogether. The instrument that should be used is a thick leather strap, which will be found quite as unpleasant as the cane, and can do no possible harm.

Health.

Deaths.

48. The health of the children has been most satisfactory. I have to report no death from either a contagious or infectious disease in a Reformatory School during the course of 1890. As regards Industrial Schools, there were only 82 deaths out of close upon 10,000 children detained in them during the year. Of these 82 deaths, 41 of them were from lung disease; but although the Influenza was raging through the country, the percentage of deaths from lung disease in these schools was lower than the previous year. The small number of fatal cases from contagious or infectious disease in Industrial Schools speaks well for the observation and care taken by the managers as regards new admissions and isolation. In this respect the convent of the Good Shepherd, Sunday's Well, Cork, and the convent at Parsonstown, in the King's County, deserve exceptional notice and high praise. These nuns have a special building separated from the school,

into which every newcomer is sent, and the new child is kept there, specially well cared for and looked after, for three weeks before being allowed to join the other children. The excellent health of the children in all these schools shows also that the sanitary arrangements are generally satisfactory. In this respect the Meath Industrial School at Blackrock, Co. Dublin, is a model institution, but this will not be wondered at considering the close care and attention given to its management, and the large portion of his valuable time placed at its disposal by Dr. Samuel Gordon.

Sanitary arrangements.

Rickets.

49. This disease, perhaps the most melancholy one that attacks the children of this country, is specially prevalent in Dublin. It consists of a weakness of the bone, and is due to the fact that the children of the poorer classes are not provided with dietary containing sufficient quantity of the salts of lime, which are absolutely necessary for the formation of bone in children. I wish to impress on managers that the highest authorities state the best treatment for weakness of the bone is to administer cod liver oil, and above all to give plenty of milk to those who suffer from it.

Ophthalmia.

50. I am sorry to say ophthalmia still continues a prevalent disease. It is exceptionally virulent just now. Where it exists those who are afflicted with it should be at once separated from the other children. Managers should also bear in mind the caution given by my distinguished predecessor, Dr. Plunkett O'Farrell, not to use atropine without, if possible, consulting a physician. I think it right moreover to call their attention to the weighty words of Mr. Swanzy on the reckless use of this very powerful alkaloid :—

"Atropine," he says, "while it is so useful in the treatment of inflammations of the iris . . . . &c., is of no benefit in many other diseases of the eye, and is *positively harmful in some of them.* It is necessary to make this statement very explicitly, for some, perhaps I should say many, medical men, who have not devoted attention to the subject of eye disease, habitually include atropine in every eyewater they prescribe. . . . . It is to be feared that the reason for this random prescribing of atropine is to be found in an ignorance of diagnosis, which leads practitioners to throw atropine, with a number of other drugs, into their eyewaters, in the hope that some of the ammunition will hit the mark wherever the latter may be." *.

* Swanzy's Handbook of Eye Diseases, p. 363

Dietary.

51. I am glad to state that, as a general rule, the dietary is fairly satisfactory. In the case of those children, however, a very generous diet is required to develop their muscular, as well as the cerebral and mental functions, and to promote the energy and vigour which can alone engender a feeling of self-reliance. It must not be forgotten that these children are for the most part taken from the street with their constitutions impaired, the circulation vitiated by bad food and exposure to hardship, and are predisposed to rickets, consumption, and scrofula in its various phases. The child of an Industrial School is adopted by the State, not because he is destitute, but lest he should fall into the criminal classes. The State stands to him "*in loco parentis*," and it is the duty of managers to prepare him physically, as well as morally, to support himself independently on his discharge from school. Hence the greatest attention ought to be given to dietary. According to the universally accepted doctrine of scientists, milk contains all the necessary elements of food for a growing child in the best form. The substances in milk are the nitrogenous matters, the fat and oil, sugar in the form of lactin, water and its salts. The lowest possible diet for a man at work should be about 6 ozs. of protoids to 14 ozs. of carbohydrates. This would be hardly sufficient for a growing child; but managers should always bear in mind that a perfect diet would be a proper mixture of nitrogenous matter and hydro-carbon, and, with that view, it may be useful to them if I print a percentage table, which I have caused to be made out, showing the component parts of some common articles of food.

—	Water.	Protoids.	Fats.	Carbo-hydrates.	Salts.
Beefsteak,	74·4	20·5	3·5	-	1·6
Fat Pork,	39·0	9·8	48·9	-	2·3
White Fish,	78·0	18·1	2·9	-	1·0
Wheaten Bread,	40·0	8·0	1·5	49·2	1·3
Rice,	10·0	5·0	0·8	83·2	0·5
Oatmeal,	15·0	12·6	5·6	63·8	3·0
Peas, Lentils, Haricot Beans, &c.	15·0	23·0	2·0	55·4	2·6
Potatoes,	74·0	2·0	0·16	21·0	1·0
Cabbage,	91·0	1·8	0·5	5·8	0·7
Eggs,	73·5	13·5	11·6	-	1·0
Milk,	86·8	4·0	3·7	4·8	0·7
Skimmed Milk,	88·0	4·0	1·8	5·4	0·8
Sugar,	3·0	-	-	96·5	0·5

This table shows what excellent food peas, lentils, beans, and oatmeal are. It will be observed also that white fish combined with rice is most nourishing, a fact that Catholic managers especially would do well to remember, and, further, how little nourishment there is in the potato, seeing that it contains per cent. 74 parts of water and only 2 of proteid. I perceive, in the dietary tables which have been furnished to me, that several managers use considerable quantities of sugar and syrup. They are right in doing so; these substances are cheap, fat-forming, and valuable in winter.

CONCLUSION.

In the early part of last year Mr. Devlin, who enjoyed the confidence of all my predecessors, was transferred from this office to the Local Government Board. His loss to the clerical staff has been much felt, but the experience and zeal of Mr. Luscombe has been of great assistance to me in the administration of this Department. I have also received valuable help from my predecessor, Dr. Geo. Plunkett O'Farrell, who at all times has been most ready to give me the benefit of his sound judgment and advice. I have to thank Mr. Colles Moore for the Appendices to this Report.

I cannot conclude without congratulating the great majority of Managers on the intelligence and caution exhibited by them in making provision for the disposal of those committed to their keeping. The success or failure of the whole Industrial School system turns largely on the diligence, prudence, and care with which this duty is discharged. If those detained in Industrial Schools, besides receiving a sound moral training and good technical instruction, get a fair start in life, then indeed there is reason to hope they may show themselves able to bear the burden of citizenship in a Free State.

I have the honour to be,

Sir,

Your obedient servant,

ROWLAND BLENNERHASSETT, BART.

Inspector.

APPENDIX.

Appendix I.

Names of Reformatory Schools.

List of Reformatory Schools in Ireland, with date of Certificate, Locality, Name of Corresponding Manager, and Sex and Religion of Young Offenders received.

County.	Name and Situation of Reformatory, Date of Certificate, and Name of Corresponding Manager.
Antrim, . .	1. Malone Reformatory School for Protestant boys, Belfast. Certified 13th March, 1860. Manager, Mr. David Barclay.
Dublin, . .	2. High Park Reformatory School for R. C. girls, Drumcondra, Dublin. Certified 21st December, 1858. Manager, Mrs. Mary Tobin.
,,*	3. Reformatory School for Protestant boys, 3, Rehoboth-place, Dublin. Certified 18th November, 1859. Official Manager, Rev. James Monahan, D.D., Rector of St. Mary's, Dublin.
,,	4. Reformatory School for Protestant girls, 105, Cook-street, Dublin. Certified 13th April, 1859. Official Manager, Rev. James Monahan, D.D., Rector of St. Mary's, Dublin.
King's Co.,† .	5. King's County Reformatory School for R. C. boys, Philipstown. Certified 22nd December, 1870. Manager, Rev. Chas. Cox.
Limerick, .	6. St. Joseph's Reformatory School for R. C. girls, Limerick. Certified 25th January, 1859. Manager, Mrs. Mary Anne Bartley.
Monaghan,‡ .	7. Spark's Lake Reformatory School for R. C. girls, Monaghan. Certified 29th July, 1859. Manager, Mrs. M. X. Finegan.
Wicklow, .	8. St. Kevin's Reformatory School for R. C. boys, Glencree, Enniskerry. Certified 12th April, 1859. Manager, Rev. John King.

* The Protestant Reformatory School for Boys at 3, Rehoboth-place, was closed in August, 1890.

† A Penal Reformatory is attached to this Institution.

‡ This Institution holds the place of a Penal Reformatory for Roman Catholic girls, and to it are transferred all those considered incorrigible in other Reformatory Schools.

LIST OF INDUSTRIAL SCHOOLS, showing locality, &c.

County.	Name and Situation of Industrial School, Date of Certificate, and Name of Corresponding Manager.	Limit fixed by Chief Secretary.
ANTRIM, . .	1. The Ulster Industrial School Training Ship *Grampian*, for Protestant boys, Belfast. Certified 22nd June, 1872. Hon. Secretary, Alfred Munster, esq., Belfast; E. A. Kerby, esq., R.N., Capt. Superintendent.	250
" . .	2. Fox Lodge, Ballynafeigh, Belfast, for young Protestant boys under 10 years of age. Certified 10th January, 1884. Hon. Sec., Alfred Munster, esq. C.M.—Wm. Patterson, esq.	100
" . .	3. Hampton House Industrial School for Protestant girls, near Belfast. Certified 13th April, 1874. C.M.—John Coates, esq.	120
" . .	4. St. Patrick's Industrial School for R. C. boys, Milltown, Belfast. This is a transfer of the certificate from the school, Donegal-street, Belfast, certified 27th August, 1869. Re-certified 11th January, 1876. C.M.—Rev. D. M'Cashin, Administrator, Belfast.	150
" . .	5. St. Patrick's Industrial School for R. C. girls, Belfast. Certified 27th August, 1869. C.M.—Rev. James Hamill, Belfast.	110
" . .	6. Shamrock Lodge, Belfast, for Protestant Girls. Certified 30th March, 1887. C.M.—Mrs. Margaret Byers.	40
ARMAGH, .	7. Middletown Industrial School for R.C. girls. Certified 21st June, 1881. C.M.—Mrs. Mary E. O'Donovan.	50
" . .	8. Lurgan Industrial School for R. C. Girls. Certified 28th April, 1888. C.M.—Mrs. Elizabeth O'Hagan.	50
CAVAN, . .	9. St. Joseph's Industrial School for R. C. girls, Cavan. Certified 1st October, 1869. C.M.—Mrs. A. M. Irwin.	67
CLARE, . .	10. Ennis Industrial School for R. C. girls. Certified 28th February, 1880. C.M.—Mrs. M. J. Perry.	60
CORK, . .	11. St. Aloysius' Industrial School for R. C. girls, Clonakilty. Certified 13th November, 1869. C.M.—Mrs. M. de S. Murray.	130
" . .	12. St. Coleman's Industrial School for R. C. girls, Queenstown. Certified 5th September, 1870. C.M.—Mrs. Maria O'Neill.	46
" . .	13. Our Lady of Mercy Industrial School for R. C. girls, Kinsale. Certified 10th November, 1869. C.M.—Mrs. M. E. Fallon.	150
" .	14. Danesfort Industrial School for R. C. boys, Upton, Co. Cork. Certified 18th April, 1889. C.M.—Rev. M. Garelli.	200

LIST OF INDUSTRIAL SCHOOLS—*continued.*

County.	Name and Situation of Industrial School, Date of Certificate, and Name of Corresponding Manager.	Limit fixed by Chief Secretary.
CORK, . .	15. St. John's Home, Union Quay, for Protestant girls. Certified 13th December, 1879. C.M.—Miss E. M. Woodroffe.	25
" . .	16. The Home Industrial School for Protestant Boys, Marble-hill, Blackrock, county Cork. This is a transfer from the school on the South-terrace, Cork, which was certified 28th July, 1871. Re-certified 25th February, 1873. C.M.—Edwin Hall, esq., Cork.	100
" . .	17. Mallow Industrial School for R. C. girls. Certified 10th April, 1890. C.M.—Mrs. M. C. Cheevers.	60
" . .	18. The Passage West Industrial School for young boys under 10 years of age, certified 27th September, 1883. C.M.—Mrs. Mary P. Murphy.	33
" . .	19. Baltimore Fishing School for R. C. boys. Certified 12th August, 1887. C.M.—Rev. C. Davis, P.P.	150
" . .	20. St. Finbar's Industrial School for R. C. girls, Sunday's Well, Cork. Certified 30th April, 1870. New Buildings re-certified for an increased number of children, 2nd December, 1872. C.M.—Mrs. Mary Devereux.	133
" . .	21. Greenmount Industrial School for R. C. boys. Certified 14th March, 1871. C.M.—Mr. R. P. Curtin.	200
" . .	22. St. Nicholas' Industrial School for Protestant boys, Cork. Certified 20th August, 1870. C.M.—Rev. George Webster, D.D., Rector of St. Nicholas', Cork.*	98
" .	23. Training Home Industrial School for Protestant girls, Union-quay, a transfer from Glanmire and Passage West school. Certified 25th October, 1870. Re-certified 14th March, 1871. C.M.—Miss Elizabeth M. Woodroffe.	50
DUBLIN, . .	24. Artane Industrial School for R. C. boys, Artane. Certified 9th July, 1870. C.M.—Rev. Thomas A. Hoope.	800
" . .	25. Booterstown Industrial School for R. C. girls, Booterstown. Certified 10th November, 1870. C.M.—Mrs. M. Hogan.	184
" . .	26. Golden Bridge Industrial School for R. C. girls. Certified 13th July, 1880. C.M.—Mrs. M. Kirwan.	150
" . .	27. The Kilmore Probationary Industrial School, Fairview, co. Dublin, for young male R. C. offenders, sent under the 13th section of the Industrial Schools Act. Certified 24th June, 1881. C.M.—Mr. Patrick C. Pigott.	100

* Dr. Webster died on 17th December, 1890, and was succeeded by the Rev. Mr. Nicholson, who was appointed manager on February 10, 1891.

LIST OF INDUSTRIAL SCHOOLS—continued.

County.	Name and Situation of Industrial School, Date of Certificate, and Name of Corresponding Manager.	Limit fixed by Chief Secretary.
DUBLIN, . .	28. St. Mary's Industrial School for R. C. girls, Lakelands, Sandymount. Certified 25th February, 1869. C.M.—Mrs. Frances Mulhall.	70
" .	29. Meath Industrial School for Protestant boys, Blackrock. Certified 5th May, 1871. C.M.—Samuel Gordon, esq., M.D., Hon. Secretary.	126
" . .	30. Merrion Industrial School for R. C. girls. Certified 10th June, 1873. C.M.—Mary Anne Baker.	150
" . .	31. Hoytesbury-street Industrial School for Protestant girls, Dublin. Certified 24th July, 1869. Jacob Geoghegan, esq., Hon. Secretary.	65
GALWAY, . .	32. St. Bridget's Industrial School for R. C. girls, Loughrea. Certified 25th November, 1869. C.M.—Mrs. Louisa Smyth.	113
" . .	33. St. Joseph's, Ballinasloe, for R. C. girls. Certified 8th July, 1884. C.M.—Mrs. M. Burke.	60
" . .	34. Clifden Industrial School for R. C. girls, Connemara. Certified 15th July, 1872. C.M.—Mrs. Mary V. Ryan.	80
" . .	35. St. Joseph's Industrial School, Letterfrack, Galway, for R. C. boys. Certified 1st April, 1886. C.M.—Mr. P. C. Flood.	130
" . .	36. Oughterard Industrial School for R. C. girls. Certified 12th May, 1873. C.M.—Mrs. Elizabeth Martyn.	40
" . .	37. St. Anne's Industrial School for R. C. girls, Galway. Certified 3rd December, 1869. C.M.—Mrs. Magdalen Blake.	77
" . .	38. Salthill Industrial School for R. C. boys. Certified September, 1871. C.M.—Mr. M. N. Roche.	200
KERRY, . .	39. St. Joseph's Home Industrial Schools, Killarney—For R. C. girls; certified 4th November, 1869. For R. C. young boys; certified 19th August, 1872. C.M.—Mrs. Mary J. E. Lombard.	103
" . .	40. St. Joseph's Industrial School for R. C. boys, Tralee. Certified 25th March, 1871. C.M.—Mr. James F. Butler.	100
" . .	41. Pembroke Alms House Industrial School for R. C. girls, Tralee. Certified 4th November, 1869. C.M.—Mrs. Mary E. O'Reardon.	70
KILKENNY, .	42. Kilkenny Industrial School for R. C. young boys. Certified 13th December, 1870. C.M.—Mrs. Sarah Byrne.	103

LIST OF INDUSTRIAL SCHOOLS—*continued.*

County.	Name and Situation of Industrial School, Date of Certificate, and Name of Corresponding Manager.	Limit fixed by Chief Secretary.
KILKENNY, .	43. Kilkenny Industrial School for R. C. girls. Certified 23nd March, 1873. C.M.—Mrs. Mary Anne Farrell.	100
KING'S, . .	44. St. John's Industrial School for R. C. girls, Parsonstown. Certified 5th July, 1870. C.M.—Mrs. Mary A. Beckett.	80
LIMERICK, .	45. St. George's Industrial School for R. C. girls, Limerick. Certified 11th December, 1869. C.M.—Mrs. Mary Anne Bartley.	80
.	46. St. Vincent's Industrial School for R. C. girls, Limerick. Certified 6th December, 1869. C.M.—Mrs. Mary A. Kenny.	130
" .	47. Limerick School for R. C. Boys. Certified 18th August, 1875. C.M.—Mr. John B. M'Donnell.	130
LONGFORD, .	48. Our Lady of Succour Industrial School for R. C. girls, Newtownforbes. Certified 29th November, 1869. C.M.—Mrs. Mary de Sales Fallon.	145
LOUTH, . .	49. House of Charity Industrial School for R. C. boys, Drogheda. Certified 17th October, 1870. C.M.—Mrs. Frances Austin.	93
" .	50. The Dundalk Industrial School for R. C. girls. Certified 12th July, 1881. C.M.—Mrs. Frances Duffy.	80
MAYO, . .	51. St. Columba Industrial School for R. C. girls, Westport. Certified 13th April, 1871. C.M.—Mrs. M. P. Cullen.	105
" .	52. St. Francis Xavier's Industrial School for R. C. girls, Ballaghaderreen. Certified 6th June, 1886. C.M.—Mrs. Merrogh-Bernard.	75
MONAGHAN, .	53. St. Martha's Industrial School for R. C. girls, Monaghan. Certified 4th November, 1869. C.M.—Mrs. M. X. Finegan.	67
ROSCOMMON, .	54. St. Monica's Industrial School for R. C. girls, Roscommon. Certified 29th November, 1869. C.M.—Mrs. M. X. Hogan.	44
" .	55. Summerhill Industrial School for R. C. girls, Athlone. Certified 17th October, 1883. C.M.—Mrs. E. Jones.	133
SLIGO, . .	56. The Banada Abbey Industrial School for R. C. girls, Tubbercurry. Certified 20th June, 1882. C.M.—Mrs. Agnes Connolly.	50
.	57. St. Lawrence Industrial School for R. C. girls, Sligo. Certified 22nd April, 1871. C.M.—Mrs. M. F. O'Beirne.	120

LIST OF INDUSTRIAL SCHOOLS—*continued.*

County.	Name and Situation of Industrial School, Date of Certificate, and Name of Corresponding Manager.	Limit fixed by Chief Secretary.
TIPPERARY, .	58. Clonmel Industrial School for R. C. boys. Certified 12th January, 1885. C.M.—Rev. T. Buckley.*	150
" .	59. St. Augustine's Industrial School for R. C. girls, Templemore. Certified 20th August, 1870. C.M.—Mrs. M. Josephine Walsh.	60
" .	60. St. Francis' Industrial School for R. C. girls, Cashel. Certified 8th December, 1869. C.M.—Mrs. M. Catherine Ryan.	110
" .	61. St. Louis' Industrial School for R. C. girls, Thurles. Certified 11th December, 1869. C.M.—Mrs. M. B. Hogan.	45
" .	62. Tipperary Industrial School for R. C. girls. Certified 1st May, 1872. C.M.—Mrs. Mary Catherine M'Namara.	64
TYRONE, . .	63. St. Catherine's Industrial School for R. C. girls, Strabane. Certified 30th November, 1869. C.M.—Mrs. Mary C. Atkinson.	100
WATERFORD, .	64. Cappoquin Industrial School for R. C. young boys. Certified 1st March, 1873. C.M.—Mrs. Margaret Devereux.	51
" .	65. St. Dominick Industrial School for R. C. girls, Waterford. Certified 13th April, 1871. C.M.—Mrs. Elizabeth Crilly.	120
WESTMEATH, .	66. Mount Carmel Industrial School for R. C. girls, Moate. Certified 9th April, 1870. C.M.—Mrs. M. Bourke.	53
WEXFORD, .	67. St. Aidan's Industrial School for R. C. girls, New Ross. Certified 13th November, 1869. C.M.—Mrs. Kate Devereux.	70
" .	68. St. Michael's Industrial School for R. C. girls, Wexford. Certified 25th November, 1869. C.M.—Mrs. M. A. Maguire.	100
WICKLOW, .	69. Meath Industrial School for Protestant girls, Bray. Certified 4th October, 1872. C.M.—Miss M'Guire.	60
" .	70. The Rathdrum Industrial School for young R. C. boys under 10 years of age. Certified 31st December, 1883. C.M.—Mrs. Margt. Tynan.	60
	TOTALS, . .	7,630

* The present manager is the Rev. M. Fennell.

	Protestants.	Roman Catholics.	Total.
Males, .	674	2,737	3,411
Females, .	340	3,775	4,115
	1,014	6,512	7,626
Mixed.			103
		Gross Total, . .	7,639

	Males.	Females.	
Protestant Schools, .	5	6	11
Roman Catholic Schools,	16	43	59
Total, ...	21	49	70

The School at St. Joseph's Home, Killarney, receives both boys and girls.

Appendix [illegible]

[illegible]

[illegible]	Boys.				Girls.				Total.		Grand Total.
	[illegible]	[illegible]	[illegible]	[illegible]	[illegible]	[illegible]	[illegible]	[illegible]	Boys.	Girls.	
[illegible]	[illegible]	[illegible]	[illegible]	[illegible]	[illegible]	[illegible]	[illegible]	[illegible]	[illegible]	[illegible]	[illegible]
Total,	[illegible]	[illegible]	[illegible]	[illegible]	[illegible]	[illegible]	[illegible]	[illegible]	[illegible]	[illegible]	[illegible]
[illegible]	[illegible]	[illegible]	[illegible]	[illegible]	[illegible]	[illegible]	[illegible]	[illegible]	[illegible]	[illegible]	[illegible]
Total,	[illegible]	[illegible]	[illegible]	[illegible]	[illegible]	[illegible]	[illegible]	[illegible]	[illegible]	[illegible]	[illegible]
[illegible]	[illegible]	[illegible]	[illegible]	[illegible]	[illegible]	[illegible]	[illegible]	[illegible]	[illegible]	[illegible]	[illegible]
[illegible]	[illegible]	[illegible]	[illegible]	[illegible]	[illegible]	[illegible]	[illegible]	[illegible]	[illegible]	[illegible]	[illegible]
Total,	[illegible]	[illegible]	[illegible]	[illegible]	[illegible]	[illegible]	[illegible]	[illegible]	[illegible]	[illegible]	[illegible]
[illegible]	[illegible]	[illegible]	[illegible]	[illegible]	[illegible]	[illegible]	[illegible]	[illegible]	[illegible]	[illegible]	[illegible]

[illegible]

[illegible]

5.—REFORMATORY SCHOOLS.—RETURN showing the Number of Admissions, Discharges, and Modes of Discharge from 1859 to 1890.

—	TOTAL. Boys.	TOTAL. Girls.	GROSS TOTAL.	—	TOTAL. Boys.	TOTAL. Girls.	GROSS TOTAL.
Admissions.				*Discharges.*			
1859, . .	96	44	140				
1860, . .	178	68	246	To employment or service,	1,558	473	2,031
1861, . .	137	59	196	To friends, ...	2,077	400	2,477
1862, . .	111	63	174	Emigrated, ...	916	155	1,071
1863, . .	119	62	181	Sent to sea, ...	137	–	137
1864, . .	139	46	185	Enlisted, ...	351	–	351
1865, . .	118	42	160	Discharged as diseased, .	46	24	70
1866, . .	166	27	193	Discharged as incorrigible or sentenced to penal servitude, . . .	45	9	54
1867, . .	164	40	204	Transferred, . . .	115	92	207
1868, . .	218	42	260	Died, ...	149	30	179
1869, . .	215	44	259	Absconded, sentence expired, ...	75	6	81
1870, . .	220	45	265				
1871, . .	235	51	286	Total, .	5,369	1,292	6,661
1872, . .	249	58	307				
1873, . .	250	44	294				
1874, . .	219	65	284				
1875, . .	198	46	244				
1876, . .	188	57	245				
1877, . .	210	65	275				
1878, . .	228	40	268				
1879, . .	221	44	265				
1880, . .	243	63	306	Under detention, 31st Dec., 1890, . . .	698	118	816
1881, . .	251	58	309	Viz.:			
1882, . .	278	41	310	In school, . . .	628	116	744
1883, . .	196	64	260	On licence, . . .	67	1	68
1884, . .	199	45	244	In prison, . . .	1	–	1
1885, . .	146	18	164	Absconded, sentence unexpired, . . .	2	–	2
1886, . .	176	30	206				
1887, . .	146	32	178				
1888, . .	165	60	225				
1889, . .	253	25	278				
1890, . .	137	19	156				
Total, .	6,068	1,410	7,478	Retained in school, sentence expired, . .	–	1	1

There was one boy admitted in November, 1889, into Philipstown School, whose sentence was expired in 1889, and who, therefore, should not have been included amongst the admissions in 1889.

C.—[illegible]

[illegible]	[illegible]	[illegible]	[illegible]	[illegible]	[illegible]	[illegible]	[illegible]	[illegible]	[illegible]	[illegible]	[illegible]
[illegible]	[illegible]	[illegible]	[illegible]	[illegible]	[illegible]	[illegible]	[illegible]	[illegible]	[illegible]	[illegible]	[illegible]
Total	[illegible]	[illegible]	[illegible]	[illegible]	[illegible]	[illegible]	[illegible]	[illegible]	[illegible]	[illegible]	[illegible]
[illegible]	[illegible]	[illegible]	[illegible]	[illegible]	[illegible]	[illegible]	[illegible]	[illegible]	[illegible]	[illegible]	[illegible]
Total	[illegible]	[illegible]	[illegible]	[illegible]	[illegible]	[illegible]	[illegible]	[illegible]	[illegible]	[illegible]	[illegible]

7.—Reformatory Schools.—Return of Receipts

Receipts and Expenditure.	Boys.			
	Belfast, Malone.	Dublin, 5, Rehoboth-place.	King's Co., Philipstown.	Wicklow Co., St. Kevin's, Glencree.
Receipts.	£ s. d.	£ s. d.	£ s. d.	£ s. d.
Treasury Allowances,	1,111 18 10	170 4 4	4,600 5 6	4,300 14 0
Subscriptions, Legacies, Donations, &c.	67 9 8	—	61 8 6	229 11 6
Payments from County and Borough Rates.	465 4 8	106 5 5	1,868 11 2	2,269 0 5
Sundries,	59 15 6	—	6 8 11	—
Total Receipts,	1,704 8 3	276 9 9	6,545 13 1	6,798 5 5
Expenditure.				
Ordinary Charges.				
Officers' Pay (Salaries and House Wages).	295 0 0	98 0 0	936 10 0	619 0 0
" Rations,	128 0 0	—	448 0 0	715 0 0
Food of Inmates,	623 13 2	48 14 6	2,347 18 6	2,447 4 8
Clothing of Inmates,	141 0 8	21 1 3	636 0 8	937 11 4
Washing, Fuel, and Light,	183 4 9	40 13 6	310 16 6	468 8 0
Repairs, Rates and Taxes,	80 18 3	5 2 11	273 13 5	464 16 9
Furniture and House Sundries,	59 9 3	2 4 7	185 5 7	929 14 2
Printing and Office Expenses,	54 2 10	2 0 0	53 5 2	88 13 9
Travelling and Police,	17 12 10	3 17 6	33 4 1	66 1 10
Medical Expenses, Funerals, &c.,	43 16 1	3 0 0	91 18 7	62 14 11
Sundries, Rewards, &c.	47 18 8	18 16 0	175 5 4	267 0 10
Total Ordinary Charges,	1,668 18 9	230 11 3	5,596 3 4	6,091 18 5
Extra Charges.				
Rent of School Premises,	65 15 7	72 10 0	88 0 0	—
Interest,	—	—	28 14 6	24 17 6
Disposal, Home,	99 12 2	14 19 6	119 13 9	106 8 7
" Emigration,	—	—	—	89 14 7
Building and Land,	—	—	178 3 9	—
Total Extra Charges,	165 7 9	87 9 6	382 12 3	221 0 8
Total Expenditure,	1,834 6 6	314 0 9	5,978 14 7	6,312 17 6
Profit (including Stock on hands and Bills).	832 8 9½	—	266 7 0	109 16 9
Loss, do. do.	—	—	—	—

[illegible] and EXPENDITURE for the year 1880.

GIRLS.				Receipts and Expenditure.
[illegible], [illegible].	Dublin, High Park.	Limerick, St. Joseph's.	Monaghan, Spark's Lake.	
£ s. d.	£ s. d.	£ s. d.	£ s. d.	**Receipts.**
167 8 8	643 11 6	462 10 8	510 2 3	Treasury Allowances.
17 8 4	13 1 3	—	—	Subscriptions, Legacies, Donations, &c.
71 14 8	302 0 11	172 13 4	230 5 3	Payments from County and Borough Rates.
—	—	—	—	Sundries.
256 2 0	960 13 8	645 5 0	740 7 6	Total Receipts.
				Expenditure.
				Ordinary Charges.
101 3 0	316 0 0	160 0 0	120 0 0	Officers' Pay (Salaries and House Wages).
11 14 4	—	—	—	Rations.
74 12 6	379 0 8	230 9 5	315 10 0	Food of Inmates.
18 12 11	85 15 7	67 14 10	90 10 6	Clothing of Inmates.
27 16 1	80 15 4	27 1 0	80 0 6	Washing, Fuel, and Light.
8 10 10	21 3 8	20 7 7	50 12 6	Repairs, Rates, and Taxes.
11 3 7	5 10 0	13 0 5	18 10 0	Furniture and House Sundries.
3 1 7	19 17 4	6 17 5	5 0 0	Printing and Office Expenses.
1 19 5	2 4 6	—	—	Travelling and Police.
8 2 4	17 13 0	15 13 8	20 10 0	Medical Expenses, Funerals, &c.
4 10 8	20 0 0	10 1 2	10 10 0	Sundries, Rewards, &c.
261 8 3	850 13 0	597 10 6	651 3 0	Total Ordinary Charges.
				Extra Charges.
35 0 0	70 0 0	40 0 0	50 0 0	Rent of School Premises.
—	—	73 0 8	33 0 0	Interest.
5 0 7	11 5 0	16 14 2	28 10 0	Disposal, Home.
—	—	4 7 8	—	" Emigration.
—	—	—	—	Building and Land.
40 0 7	81 5 0	134 0 8	111 10 0	Total Extra Charges.
301 8 10	934 3 0	732 6 0	762 13 0	Total Expenditure.
20 11 9	138 1 4	66 15 0	34 0 5	Profit (including Stock on hands and Bills).
—	—	—	—	Loss, &c.

[illegible].—Reformatory Schools.—Summary showing Expenditure and Cost per Head for the Year [illegible].

Reformatory Schools.	[illegible]	[illegible]	[illegible]	Gross Total of Expenditure.	[illegible]	Net Cost of Expenditure.	Average Number of [illegible]	Net Cost per [illegible] per annum.
	£ s. d.	£ s. d.	£ s. d.	£ s. d.	£ s. d.	£ s. d.		£ s. d.
[illegible]	[illegible]	[illegible]	[illegible]	[illegible]	[illegible]	[illegible]	[illegible]	[illegible]
[illegible]	[illegible]	[illegible]	[illegible]	[illegible]	—	[illegible]	[illegible]	[illegible]
[illegible]	[illegible]	[illegible]	[illegible]	[illegible]	[illegible]	[illegible]	[illegible]	[illegible]
[illegible]	[illegible]	[illegible]	[illegible]	[illegible]	[illegible]	[illegible]	[illegible]	[illegible]
[illegible]	[illegible]	[illegible]	[illegible]	[illegible]	[illegible]	[illegible]	[illegible]	[illegible]
[illegible]	[illegible]	[illegible]	[illegible]	[illegible]	[illegible]	[illegible]	[illegible]	[illegible]
[illegible]	[illegible]	[illegible]	[illegible]	[illegible]	[illegible]	[illegible]	[illegible]	[illegible]
[illegible]	[illegible]	[illegible]	[illegible]	[illegible]	[illegible]	[illegible]	[illegible]	[illegible]
	[illegible]	[illegible]	[illegible]	[illegible]	[illegible]	[illegible]	—	—

INDUSTRIAL SCHOOLS.

8.—Industrial Schools.—Return of Admissions,

	[illegible] Training Ship, Belfast.	Fox Lodge, Belfast.	Hampton K[illegible], Belfast.	St. Patrick's, Milltown, Belfast.	St. Patrick's, Crumlin-road, Belfast.	Shamrock Lodge, Belfast.	Middletown, co. Armagh.	Lurgan.	St. Joseph's, Derry.	[illegible].	St. Aloysius, Clonakilty.	St. Colman's, Queenstown.	Our Lady of Mercy, Kinsale.	[illegible], Upton, Cork.	St. John's Home, Water Grass[illegible].	Boys' Home, [illegible], Blackrock-road.	Mallow.
	B.	B.	G.	B.	G.	G.	G.	G.	G.	B.	B.	G.	G.	B.	G.	B.	G.
Under Detention, 31st Dec., 1889:— In School (within number paid for under rules),	229	100	99	150	11[illegible]	40	50	50	87	80	130	48	160	151	18	44	86
„ (in excess of number paid for, or under 6 years),	–	5	–	2	18	–	8	8	9	2	5	–	7	–	–	–	2
On Licence,	18	1	12	3	31	2	8	–	18	5	1	5	6	–	5	1	4
Absconded, Sentence unexpired,	–	–	–	–	–	–	–	–	–	–	–	–	–	–	–	–	–
Retained in School, Sentence expired,	–	–	–	–	–	–	1	–	–	–	5	–	–	–	–	[illegible]	1
Total,	248	106	111	155	158	42	60	62	108	87	142	51	169	151	23	51	9[illegible]
Admitted by Committal in 1890,	58	15	26	24	28	7	20	2	6	14	13	0	22	48	–	11	12
„ Transfer,	8	1	–	–	–	–	–	–	–	–	–	–	–	14	2	–	–
„ Re-committal,	–	–	–	–	–	–	1	–	–	–	1	–	–	–	–	–	5
Total,	72	16	26	24	28	7	21	2	6	14	14	6	22	62	2	11	12
Discharged, Transferred, or Died in 1890,	58	11	18	22	18	7	11	1	12	14	14	4	20	5	4	6	9
Under Detention, 31st Dec., 1890:— In School (within number paid for under rules),	230	100	108	150	11[illegible]	41	50	50	88	80	130	48	160	200	17	88	60
„ (In excess of number paid for, or under 6 years),	–	7	–	2	2[illegible]	–	12	8	–	1	8	–	8	8	–	–	16
On Licence,	31	4	13	1	16	1	8	–	10	4	–	7	10	2	2	1	5
Absconded, Sentence unexpired,	1	–	–	–	–	–	–	–	–	–	–	–	–	–	–	–	–
Retained in School, Sentence expired,	–	–	–	–	3	–	1	–	2	1	4	–	–	–	–	1	–
Total,	272	111	112	153	141	42	69	59	100	86	142	55	180	20[illegible]	19	90	77
Average Number of Children, (i.) Inmates under orders of Detention and paid for by Treasury.	240	100	99	150	118	39	50	50	80	80	130	48	150	191	18	51	80
(ii.) Inmates under Orders of Detention but as yet not chargeable to the Treasury, being under 6 years of age.	–	5	–	–	–	2	4	–	–	–	1	–	4	2	–	1	1
(iii.) Inmates above the age of 6 years under Orders of Detention, but as yet not chargeable to the Treasury, being in excess of the number limited by the rules of the School.	–	–	–	1	18	–	6	3	–	2	8	–	6	–	–	–	9
(iv.) Voluntary Inmates (Inmates not under Orders of Detention) supported by the Managers out of funds other than those received from the Treasury.	–	–	4	8	28	–	2	–	6	–	7	3	–	–	10	4	6
Total,	242	105	108	158	158	41	64	58	90	82	143	68	166	193	28	60	104
Average Number of Externs attending the School.	–	–	–	–	–	5	106	–	–	822	–	500	–	–	3	–	204

Disposition, &c. for Year [illegible]

[illegible]

8.—INDUSTRIAL SCHOOLS.—RETURN of ADMISSIONS,

—	St. Joseph's, Tralee.	Pembroke Alms-house, Tralee.	Kilkenny Male.	Kilkenny Female.	St. John's, [illegible].	St. Joseph's, Limerick.	St. Vincent's, Limerick.	Limerick Male.	Our Lady of Succour, N. T. Forbes.	House of Charity, Drogheda.	Dundalk.
	Boys.	G.	B.	G.	G.	Girls.	Girls.	Boys.	Girls.	Boys.	Girls.
Under Detention, 31st Dec., 1879:—											
In School (within number paid for under rules).	96	78	162	100	80	90	130	148	145	93	82
" (In excess of number paid for, or under 6 years).	—	—	—	4	2	13	8	—	4	8	1
On License,	6	11	13	11	6	4	19	24	5	7	8
Absconded, Sentence unexpired,	1	—	—	—	—	—	—	—	—	—	—
Retained in School, Sentence expired,	—	2	—	—	1	—	11	1	—	—	8
Total,	103	88	175	115	91	103	168	173	152	107	9[illegible]
Admitted by Commitment in 1880,	16	17	37	14	8	7	42	30	28	13	13
" Transfer,	3	—	—	—	—	—	—	1	—	—	—
" Re-committal,	—	—	—	—	—	—	2	—	—	—	—
Total,	19	17	37	14	8	7	48	31	28	13	18
Discharged, Transferred, or died in 1880,	16	19	38	18	8	11	36	35	28	17	18
Under Detention, 31st Dec., 1880:—											
In School (within number paid for under rules).	99	69	158	100	80	80	130	140	148	92	80
" (In excess of number paid for, or under 6 years).	—	2	1	3	4	15	13	—	6	4	5
On License,	6	13	15	6	6	3	28	31	7	2	8
Absconded, Sentence unexpired,	2	—	—	—	—	—	—	—	—	—	—
Retained in School, Sentence expired,	—	4	—	—	1	1	9	1	—	—	8
Total,	106	88	174	112	90	99	178	171	158	103	93
AVERAGE NUMBER OF CHILDREN.											
(i.) Inmates under orders of Detention, and paid for by Treasury.	100	70	162	100	78	80	130	142	145	92	80
(ii.) Inmates under Orders of Detention but as yet not chargeable to the Treasury, being under 6 years of age.	—	2	1	—	2	10	4	—	1	2	3
(iii.) Inmates above the age of 6 years under Orders of Detention, but as yet not chargeable to the Treasury, being in excess of the number limited by the rules of the School.	—	—	—	2	1	—	18	—	6	3	6
(iv.) Voluntary Inmates (Inmates not under Orders of Detention), supported by the Managers out of funds other than those received from the Treasury,	—	4	1	—	—	—	84	3	2	2	2
Total,	100	76	164	102	81	90	236	152	168	99	103
Average Number of Externs attending the School,	—	181	—	—	380	—	160	—	65	—	72

9.—Industrial Schools.—Summary of Admissions, Discharges, &c., for the year ending 31st December, 1890.

—	Total, Boys.	Total, Girls.	Gross Total.
Under Detention, 31st December, 1889—			
In School (within number paid for under Rules),	3,314	4,135	7,449
" (in excess of number paid for, or under 6 years of age).	20	105	125
On Licence,	330	418	748
Absconded, Sentence unexpired,	6	1	7
Retained in School, Sentence expired,	11	10	21
Total,	3,681	4,669	8,350
Admitted in 1890,	650	781	1,431
" by Transfer,	20	3	23
" by Re-committal,	7	3	10
Total,	677	787	1,464
Discharged, Transferred, or Died in 1890,	845	697	1,542
Under Detention, 31st December, 1890—			
In School (within number paid for under Rules),	3,307	4,180	7,487
" (in excess of number paid for, or under 6 years).	92	208	300
On Licence,	323	431	754
Absconded, Sentence unexpired,	8	—	8
Retained in School, Sentence expired,	5	73	78
Total,	3,735	4,892	8,627
State of Instruction on Admission—			
Neither Read nor Write,	372	319	691
Read, or Read and Write imperfectly,	240	414	654
Read and Write well,	38	46	84
Superior Instruction,	—	1	1
Total,	650	781	1,431
Age on Admission—			
Under 6 years,	3	43	46
From 6 to 8,	117	220	337
" 8 to 10,	181	214	395
" 10 to 12,	216	157	373
" 12 to 14,	133	140	273
Total,	650	781	1,431
Mode of Discharge—			
To employment or service,	315	400	715
Returned to Friends,	183	150	333
Emigrated,	27	45	72
Sent to Sea,	9	—	9
Enlisted,	6	—	6
Specially discharged,	13	5	18
Committed to Reformatory,	7	1	8
Transfers,	101	3	104
Died,	27	55	82
Absconders discharged by expiration of sentence,	3	1	4
Discharged on account of insufficient grounds for detention.	6	10	16
Total,	845	697	1,542

10.—INDUSTRIAL SCHOOLS.—RETURN of PARTICULARS of ADMISSIONS and DISCHARGES, for the Year 1890.

—	"Grampian" Training Ship, Belfast.	Fox Lodge, Belfast.	Hampton House, Belfast.	St. Patrick's, Milltown, Belfast.	St. Patrick's, Crumlin Road, Belfast.	Shamrock Lodge, Belfast.	Middletown, co. Armagh.	Lurgan.	St. Joseph's, Cavan.	Ennis.	St. Aloysius', Clonakilty.	St. Coleman's, Queenstown.	Our Lady of Mercy, Kinsale.	Desmond, Upton, co. Cork.	St. John's Home, Union Quay.	Boys' Home, Marble-Hill, Blarney, Cork.	Mallow.	Passage West.	Baltimore, co. Cork.	St. Finbarr's, Sunday's Well, Cork.	Greenmount, Cork.	St. Vincent's, Cove-street, Cork.	Training Home, Union Quay, Cork.	Artane, co. Dublin.
	B.	B.	G.	B.	G.	G.	G.	G.	G.	G.	G.	G.	G.	B.	G.	B.	G.	B.	B.	G.	B.	B.	G.	B.
STATE OF INSTRUCTION ON ADMISSION—																								
Neither Read nor Write,	33	11	14	8	15	6	12	2	4	6	11	6	19	24	-	8	6	6	28	22	21	4	6	78
Read or Write imperfectly.	17	4	6	13	13	1	7	-	2	5	1	1	7	30	-	5	6	1	18	7	14	1	9	62
Read and Write well,	12	-	4	3	-	-	1	-	-	-	-	-	-	1	-	-	1	-	6	-	1	1	-	4
Superior Instruction,	-	-	-	-	-	-	-	-	-	-	-	-	-	-	-	-	-	-	-	-	-	-	-	-
Total,	62	15	20	24	28	7	20	2	6	14	12	6	26	45	-	11	12	7	47	29	36	6	15	141
AGE AT ADMISSION—																								
Under 6 years,	-	-	-	-	-	2	2	-	-	-	1	-	2	-	-	1	2	1	1	2	-	-	1	1
From 6 to 8,	-	9	8	1	5	3	2	-	2	-	6	4	2	4	-	2	3	5	6	4	2	6	8	4
" 8 to 10,	8	6	5	8	10	1	[illegible]	1	3	6	5	2	7	18	-	5	8	1	14	11	10	-	2	44
" 10 to 12,	28	-	7	9	7	1	5	1	[illegible]	6	4	-	8	12	-	1	3	-	18	5	16	2	8	53
" 12 to 14,	22	-	5	5	4	1	5	-	-	5	2	-	8	8	-	2	1	-	8	6	2	1	2	42
Total,	66	15	20	24	28	7	20	2	6	14	12	6	26	45	-	11	12	7	47	29	36	6	15	144
MODE OF DISCHARGE—																								
To Employment or Service.	26	-	12	20	6	7	4	1	6	11	6	2	7	-	8	6	5	-	-	[illegible]	[illegible]	2	6	155
Returned to Friends,	5	-	4	3	8	-	4	-	4	2	5	5	7	-	1	1	1	-	8	2	16	6	2	24
Emigrated,	1	1	-	2	-	-	1	-	2	-	1	-	1	1	-	2	-	-	1	6	-	-	-	6
Sent to Sea,	5	-	-	-	-	-	-	-	-	-	-	-	-	-	-	-	-	-	-	-	-	-	-	-
Enlisted,	-	-	-	-	-	-	-	-	-	-	-	-	-	-	-	-	-	-	-	-	-	-	-	5
Specially discharged,	5	-	-	-	-	-	-	-	-	-	-	-	-	2	-	-	1	-	-	-	1	-	-	6
Committed to Reformatory.	6	1	-	-	-	-	-	-	-	-	-	-	-	-	-	-	-	-	-	-	1	-	-	-
Transferred,	1	5	-	-	-	-	-	-	-	-	-	-	-	-	-	-	-	8	-	-	-	-	2	-
Died,	6	4	2	2	2	-	1	-	-	2	1	-	5	1	-	2	2	-	-	1	2	-	-	8
Absconders discharged by expiration of sentence.	-	-	-	-	-	-	-	-	-	-	-	-	-	-	-	-	-	-	-	-	1	-	1	2
Discharged on account of insufficient grounds for Detention.	-	-	-	-	-	-	1	-	-	-	1	-	-	1	-	-	-	-	8	-	-	-	-	1
Total,	66	11	16	25	16	7	11	1	11	15	14	4	20	6	4	6	6	6	7	31	40	11	15	195

10.—Industrial Schools.—Return of Particulars of Admission

—	Booterstown, co. Dublin.	Golden Bridge.	[illegible] Protestant Industrial School, co. Dublin.	St. Mary's, Lakelands, Sandymount, co. Dublin.	Meath, Blackrock, co. Dublin.	[illegible], co. Dublin.	[illegible], Dublin.	St. Bridget's, [illegible].	[illegible]	Clifden, co. Galway.	Letterfrack.	Oughterard, co. Galway.	St. Anne's, Galway.	Salt Hill, Galway.	St. Joseph's Home, Kilkenny.		St. Joseph's, Tralee.	[illegible], Tralee.	Killarney Male.	Killarney Female.	St. Joseph's, [illegible].
	G.	G.	B.	G.	B.	G.	G.	G.	G.	G.	B.	G.	G.	B.	B.	G.	B.	G.	B.	G.	B.
State of Instruction on Admission—																					
Neither Read nor Write,	10	28	10	10	8	21	2	10	12	11	8	9	8	41	8	8	4	11	49	8	6
Read or Write imperfectly,	9	9	4	4	8	4	2	7	8	1	6	2	6	11	–	7	8	6	18	4	3
Read and Write well,	6	–	–	–	3	–	–	–	–	–	–	–	3	1	–	–	4	–	–	3	–
Superior Instruction,	–	–	–	–	–	–	–	–	–	–	–	–	–	–	–	–	–	–	–	–	–
Total,	25	31	14	14	16	25	4	18	18	12	10	6	17	53	8	15	16	17	67	15	9
Age at Admission—																					
Under 6 years,	–	–	–	1	–	–	–	–	–	4	–	–	1	–	–	–	–	2	1	–	[illegible]
From 6 to 8,	6	7	1	4	5	5	1	10	7	5	3	2	2	6	2	4	–	4	15	[illegible]	[illegible]
„ 8 to 10,	7	10	5	5	6	11	–	6	6	2	2	2	2	20	–	5	8	6	17	[illegible]	–
„ 10 to 12,	8	8	5	5	5	7	2	10	1	1	7	1	0	24	–	4	3	5	–	[illegible]	[illegible]
„ 12 to 14,	4	6	3	1	5	3	2	1	2	–	–	–	6	3	–	2	5	1	–	4	–
Total,	25	30	14	14	15	25	4	18	18	12	10	6	17	53	8	15	16	17	37	15	9
Mode of Discharge—																					
To Employment or Service,	15	11	15	1	14	24	2	11	5	4	1	1	7	15	–	5	9	4	–	19	7
Restored to Friends,	1	9	1	7	3	7	1	7	9	3	2	2	6	14	–	3	10	5	2	6	2
Emigrated,	1	8	1	1	–	–	–	4	1	3	–	1	1	8	1	2	3	5	–	–	–
Sent to Sea,	–	–	–	–	–	–	–	–	–	–	–	–	–	1	–	–	–	–	–	–	–
Enlisted,	–	–	1	–	–	–	–	–	–	–	2	–	–	–	–	–	–	–	–	–	–
Specially discharged,	–	–	–	–	–	–	–	–	–	–	–	–	–	–	–	–	1	–	1	–	–
Committed to Reformatory,	–	–	2	–	–	–	–	–	–	–	–	–	–	–	–	–	–	–	–	–	–
Transferred,	–	–	–	–	–	–	–	–	–	–	–	–	1	–	8	–	–	–	34	–	–
Died,	1	2	–	–	1	2	1	1	2	1	–	–	1	4	–	–	1	–	–	–	–
Absconders discharged by expiration of sentence,	–	–	–	–	–	–	–	–	–	–	–	–	–	–	–	–	–	–	–	–	–
Discharged on account of insufficient grounds for detention,	–	–	–	–	–	–	–	–	–	–	–	–	–	1	–	–	–	–	–	–	–
Total,	17	30	23	9	17	33	4	23	10	10	5	4	15	50	4	11	18	12	34	19	9

11.—Industrial Schools.—Return showing the Number of Admissions, Discharges, and Modes of Discharge, from 1869 to 1890.

—	Total, Boys.	Total, Girls.	Grand Total.
Admissions.			
1869, . . .	65	184	310
1870, . . .	258	1,171	1,429
1871, . . .	490	673	1,163
1872, . . .	788	850	1,624
1873, . . .	487	657	1,144
1874, . . .	495	561	1,056
1875, . . .	490	513	1,003
1876, . . .	367	496	863
1877, . . .	349	596	945
1878, . . .	366	499	865
1879, . . .	603	577	1,180
1880, . . .	774	830	1,604
1881, . . .	524	733	1,257
1882, . . .	611	755	1,366
1883, . . .	478	708	1,186
1884, . . .	601	703	1,304
1885, . . .	963	755	1,718
1886, . . .	753	606	1,359
1887, . . .	862	685	1,547
1888, . . .	666	771	1,437
1889, . . .	937	711	1,648
1890, . . .	882	759	1,641
Total, . .	12,579	15,110	27,689

—	Total, Boys.	Total, Girls.	Grand Total.
Discharges.			
To employment or service,	3,518	5,517	9,035
To friends, . . .	1,603	2,280	3,883
Emigrated, . . .	631	696	1,327
Sent to sea, . . .	881	-	881
Enlisted, . . .	109	-	109
Discharged as diseased, .	211	134	345
Committed to reformatories, . . .	110	53	163
Transferred, . . .	1,383	808	2,191
Died, ...	495	795	1,290
Absconded—sentence expired, ...	64	7	71
Discharged — committal illegal, . . .	128	255	383
Total, . .	9,867	10,808	18,675
Under detention, 31st Dec., 1890, . .	3,705	4,904	8,609
Viz.:—			
In school, . .	3,359	4,438	7,797
On licence, . .	323	445	768
Absconded — sentence unexpired, . .	8	-	8
Retained in school—sentence expired, .	5	73	78

12.—Industrial Schools.—Discharges for the years 1887, 1888, 1889, showing the number Doing Well, Convicted of Crime, &c., from their Discharge to 31st December, 1890.*

—	"[illegible]" Ship.	[illegible] Lodge, Belfast.	[illegible]	[illegible], Belfast.	Crumlin-road, Belfast.	[illegible]	[illegible]	[illegible]	[illegible]	[illegible]	[illegible]	St. [illegible], Cork.	[illegible] Hill, Cork.	[illegible]
Mode of Discharge—														
To Employment,	90	1	23	61	27	6	20	29	16	9	16	6	22	30
Returned to Friends,	50	2	7	14	26	4	7	11	29	5	15	6	9	6
Emigrated,	2	1	–	2	4	3	–	7	11	4	10	–	4	3
Sent to Sea,	10	–	–	–	–	–	–	–	–	–	–	–	–	–
Enlisted,	4	–	–	–	–	–	–	–	–	–	–	–	–	–
Specially Discharged,	12	–	–	2	–	–	–	–	2	–	1	–	–	1
Absconded and not Recovered,	1	–	–	–	–	–	–	–	–	–	–	–	–	–
Total,	162	4	30	86	57	11	27	47	58	18	25	12	35	40
Subsequent Character—														
Since Dead,	7	–	2	5	–	–	–	–	–	–	5	–	–	–
Doing well,	114	3	33	79	57	10	26	47	58	14	20	12	34	38
Doubtful,	7	–	2	1	–	–	–	–	–	–	–	–	–	–
Convicted of Crime,	–	–	–	–	–	–	–	–	–	–	–	–	–	–
Unknown,	34	1	–	1	–	1	1	–	–	4	3	–	1	1
Recommitted to an Industrial School,	–	–	–	–	–	–	–	–	–	–	–	–	–	1
Total,	162	4	36	86	57	11	27	47	58	18	25	12	35	40

—	[illegible] Wood.	[illegible]	[illegible] Well, Cork.	[illegible], Cork.	St. [illegible], Cork.	Training Home, Cork.	[illegible]	[illegible]	[illegible]	[illegible]	[illegible]	"[illegible]" [illegible]	[illegible]	[illegible], Dublin.
Mode of Discharge—														
To Employment,	–	–	37	53	13	15	468	41	28	–	19	41	43	21
Returned to Friends,	4	2	5	35	23	–	61	18	20	–	16	6	10	5
Emigrated,	–	1	15	20	–	–	24	4	3	–	–	7	1	–
Sent to Sea,	–	–	–	1	3	–	–	–	–	–	–	1	–	–
Enlisted,	–	–	–	–	–	–	6	–	–	1	–	–	–	–
Specially Discharged,	–	10	–	1	–	–	17	–	–	2	–	1	–	–
Absconded and not Recovered,	–	–	–	–	–	–	5	–	–	–	–	–	–	–
Total,	4	13	57	85	38	15	546	58	51	3	35	58	55	26
Subsequent Character—														
Since Dead,	–	–	1	3	–	–	4	2	3	–	2	1	3	–
Doing well,	4	3	55	81	26	15	534	56	48	3	32	49	50	20
Doubtful,	–	–	1	4	6	–	–	–	–	–	1	2	–	3
Convicted of Crime,	–	–	–	2	–	–	–	–	–	–	–	1	–	–
Unknown,	–	10	–	5	4	–	8	–	–	–	–	5	1	1
Recommitted to an Industrial School,	–	–	–	1	–	–	–	–	–	–	–	–	–	–
Total,	4	13	57	95	38	15	546	58	51	3	35	58	55	26

* There were no discharges during the 3 years of 1887-88-89 from Shamrock Lodge, Lurgan, and [illegible] Industrial Schools.

13.—Industrial Schools.—Discharges for the years 1887, 1888, 1889, showing
31st December,

—	Loughrea.	Ballinasloe.	Clifden.	Letterfrack.	Oughterard.	St. Anne's, Galway.	Salt Hill, Galway.	Killarney.	St. Joseph's, Tralee.	Pembroke Alms, Tralee.	Kilkenny, Boys.
Mode of Discharge—											
To Employment,	34	11	8	–	11	18	51	22	5	21	–
Returned to Friends,	18	2	11	–	8	10	30	6	43	7	20
Emigrated,	7	1	5	–	8	6	10	12	12	10	3
Sent to Sea,	–	–	–	–	–	–	1	–	–	–	–
Enlisted,	–	–	–	–	–	–	2	–	–	–	–
Specially Discharged,	–	–	–	2	2	1	–	–	–	–	4
Absconded and not Recovered,	–	–	–	–	–	–	1	–	1	–	–
Total,	59	14	24	2	30	44	95	40	61	38	27
Subsequent Character—											
Since Dead,	2	–	–	1	2	3	–	–	5	–	–
Doing well,	57	14	24	–	24	41	88	37	42	36	21
Doubtful,	–	–	–	–	–	1	7	1	2	1	6
Convicted of Crime,	–	–	–	–	–	–	–	–	–	–	–
Unknown,	–	–	–	1	–	–	–	2	12	1	–
Recommitted to an Industrial School.	–	–	–	–	–	–	–		–	–	–
Total,	59	14	24	2	29	44	95	40	61	38	27

—	Roscommon.	Summerhill, Girls.	Boyle Abbey.	Sligo.	Clonmel.	Templemore.	Cashel.	Thurles.	Tipperary.	Kinsale.	Cappoquin.	Waterford.
Mode of Discharge—												
To Employment,	15	31	31	22	19	19	31	26	16	45	–	47
Returned to Friends,	8	25	4	18	28	13	18	4	7	11	–	6
Emigrated,	4	9	–	–	5	–	5	3	5	4	–	8
Sent to Sea,	–	–	–	–	–	–	–	–	–	–	–	–
Enlisted,	–	–	–	–	2	–	–	–	–	–	–	–
Specially Discharged,	2	–	1	4	2	–	7	–	–	1	–	–
Absconded and not Recovered,	–	–	–	–	–	–	–	–	–	–	–	–
Total,	29	65	36	45	55	32	55	33	28	61	–	61
Subsequent Character—												
Since Dead,	1	1	4	1	1	–	2	–	–	1	–	1
Doing well,	26	60	32	42	50	32	51	33	26	59	–	60
Doubtful,	1	1	–	1	–	–	–	–	1	–	–	–
Convicted of Crime,	–	–	–	–	–	–	–	–	–	–	–	–
Unknown,	1	3	–	1	4	–	2	–	1	1	–	–
Recommitted to an Industrial School.	–	–	–	–	–	–	–	–	–	–	–	–
Total,	29	65	36	45	55	32	55	33	28	61	–	61

the number Doing Well, Convicted of Crime, &c., from their Discharge to 1910—*continued.*

Kilkenny, St. [illegible]	[illegible]	St George's, Limerick.	St. Vincent's, Limerick.	Limerick Male.	[illegible]	Dingle.	Dundalk.	Westport.	Ballaghaderreen.	Monaghan.	—
											MODE OF DISCHARGE—
36	24	18	16	71	19	1	10	19	8	21	To Employment.
11	10	11	33	20	14	4	2	6	4	13	Returned to Friends.
2	2	2	18	4	3	–	1	15	2	1	Emigrated.
–	–	–	–	–	–	–	–	–	–	–	Sent to Sea.
–	–	–	–	–	–	–	–	–	–	–	Enlisted.
–	–	–	2	4	–	–	–	–	1	–	Specially Discharged.
–	–	–	–	2	–	–	–	–	–	–	Absconded and not Recovered.
49	36	31	69	100	36	5	13	40	12	35	Total.
											SUBSEQUENT CHARACTER—
2	2	–	3	8	1	–	–	3	1	1	Since Dead.
35	33	27	55	81	24	1	13	37	9	33	Doing well.
1	1	–	–	2	3	–	–	–	1	1	Doubtful.
–	–	–	–	–	–	–	–	–	–	–	Convicted of Crime.
10	1	4	11	11	11	4	–	–	1	–	Unknown.
–	–	–	–	–	–	–	–	–	–	–	Recommitted to an Industrial School.
49	36	31	69	100	36	5	13	40	12	35	Total.

Meath.	[illegible]	Wexford.	[illegible]	[illegible]	Total.		Grand Total.	—
					Boys.	Girls.		
								MODE OF DISCHARGE—
17	49	50	12	–	842	1,087	1,927	To Employment.
6	12	10	4	1	345	201	834	Returned to Friends.
2	2	–	1	–	96	203	299	Emigrated.
–	–	–	–	–	36	–	36	Sent to Sea.
–	–	–	–	–	16	–	16	Enlisted.
2	–	–	1	–	81	28	89	Specially Discharged.
–	–	–	–	–	10	–	10	Absconded and not Recovered.
27	63	60	18	1	1,392	1,819	3,211	Total.
								SUBSEQUENT CHARACTER—
1	–	2	2	–	29	54	83	Since Dead.
23	63	58	11	–	1,234	1,678	2,902	Doing well.
1	–	–	–	–	36	20	56	Doubtful.
–	–	–	–	–	3	–	3	Convicted of Crime.
2	–	–	5	1	89	68	163	Unknown.
–	–	–	–	–	1	1	2	Recommitted to an Industrial School.
27	63	60	18	1	1,392	1,819	3,211	Total.

13.—Industrial Schools.—Return of Receipts

Receipts and Expenditure.	"Grampian"* Training Ship, Belfast. Boys.	Fox Lodge, Belfast. Boys.	Hampton House, Belfast. Girls.	St. Patrick's, Milltown, Belfast. Boys.	St. Patrick's, Crumlin-road, Belfast. Girls.
	1.	2.	3.	4.	5.
Average Number of Children paid for by Treasury.	243	100	90	180	110
Average Number of Children under 6 years of age, and not yet paid for by Treasury.	–	–	–	–	
Average Number of Children in excess of limit, and not yet paid for by Treasury.	–	5·6	–	1·7	13
Average Number of Voluntary Inmates.	–	–	4	5	19
Receipts.	£ s. d.	£ s. d.	£ s. d.	£ s. d.	£ s. d.
Treasury Allowances,	3,109 10 3	1,306 3 0	1,384 9 0	1,354 19 8	1,439 13 4
Subscriptions, Legacies, Donations, &c.	857 19 0	25 6 0	0 1 0	5 0 0	634 18 [illegible]
Payments from County and Borough Rates.	1,458 8 4	687 9 9	667 3 11	903 8 8	639 8 [illegible]
Payments for Voluntary Inmates.	–	–	–	–	–
Hire of Labour,	–	–	–	–	–
Sundries,	54 15 0	–	90 9 8	4 8 0	–
Total Receipts,	5,010 7 7	1,966 11 3	1,987 0 7	2,265 9 11	2,705 18 [illegible]
Expenditure.					
Ordinary Charges.					
Officers' Pay (Salaries & House Wages).	1,464 5 10	298 16 0	110 16 6	291 10 6	190 0 0
Officers' Rations,	110 0 0	90 0 0	100 0 0	91 4 [illegible]	148 0 0
Food for Inmates,	1,565 18 6	696 12 6	490 5 6	1,060 19 6	1,140 6 6
Clothing for Inmates,	579 18 6	254 5 6	179 7 0	284 5 0	678 10 6
Washing, Fuel, and Light,	289 17 3	179 8 5	219 1 4	69 10 8	189 16 6
Repairs, Rates, and Taxes,	82 10 3	38 18 6	65 1 1	849 8 11	131 10 7
Furniture and House Sundries,	196 9 10	118 5 4	149 10 6	182 8 4	158 10 6
Printing and Office Expenses,	246 5 10	45 4 7	19 16 1	20 19 5	11 0 0
Travelling and Police Charges,	4 7 6	6 1 10	23 10 11	5 1 9	5 10 0
Medical Expenses, Funerals, &c.,	147 15 11	40 1 1	89 5 9	58 11 7	20 0 6
Sundries, Rewards, &c.,	90 10 4	40 0 0	27 9 9	55 18 4	44 10 6
Total Ordinary Charges,	4,700 10 9	1,605 13 8	1,424 9 7	2,403 15 8	2,360 1 6
Extra Charges.					
Rent of School Premises,	–	–	181 12 6	80 0 0	80 0 0
Interest,	–	9 6 5	–	–	170 0 0
Disposal, Home,	136 15 8	–	63 0 0	89 15 6	115 15 8
" Emigration and Passages,	–	–	–	7 10 0	–
Building and Land,	310 11 7	–	1,060 9 7	–	100 0 0
Total Extra Charges,	456 6 10	9 6 5	1,254 15 1	97 5 6	585 15 8
Total Expenditure,	5,157 6 7	1,675 1 7	2,679 4 8	2,500 0 [illegible]	[illegible] 15 0
Industrial Department.					
Profit (including Stock on hand and Bills).	–	–	146 19 10	81 15 5	–
Loss, do.,	–	84 8 9	–	–	0 15 7

* Repairs to ships and boats.

in, and EXPENDITURE for, the Year 1890.

Shamrock Lodge, Belfast. Girls.	Middletown, Armagh. Girls.	Lurgan. Girls.	St. Joseph's, Cavan. Girls.	[illegible]. Girls.	Receipts and Expenditure.
6.	7.	8.	9.	10.	
59	50	60	80	80	Average Number of Children paid for by Treasury.
2	4	–	–	–	Average Number of Children under 6 years of age, and not yet paid for by Treasury.
–	8	8	–	3	Average Number of Children in excess of limit, and not yet paid for by Treasury.
–	2	–	4	–	Average Number of Voluntary Inmates.
£ s. d.	£ s. d.	£ s. d.	£ s. d.	£ s. d.	RECEIPTS.
514 12 4	633 15 0	651 10 8	1,128 16 3	1,013 17 6	Treasury Allowances.
–	15 0 0	8 12 6	71 18 2	–	Subscriptions, Legacies, Donations, &c.
267 0 8	265 18 2	245 15 9	188 9 7	404 6 6	Payments from County and Borough Rates.
–	6 0 0	–	20 0 0	–	Payments for Voluntary Inmates.
–	–	–	–	–	Hire of Labour.
–	–	–	–	–	Sundries.
781 13 4	941 8 2	904 18 9	1,836 1 0	1,447 4 0	Total Receipts.
					EXPENDITURE.
					Ordinary Charges.
64 6 0	45 0 0	40 0 0	100 0 0	89 0 0	Officers' Pay (Salaries & House Wages).
40 0 0	–	72 0 0	82 10 0	76 5 0	Officers' Rations.
268 12 2½	470 5 8	433 2 8	603 14 0	605 17 11	Food for Inmates.
139 11 5	150 6 0	144 1 8	169 13 4	228 14 10	Clothing of Inmates.
108 14 1	140 16 0	85 0 0	200 0 0	188 17 9	Washing, Fuel, and Light.
23 11 3	34 14 9	31 19 1	134 0 7	81 19 5	Repairs, Rates, and Taxes.
38 12 7	35 18 4	28 10 0	67 15 3	27 7 6	Furniture and House Sundries.
17 4 2	33 18 9	15 13 0	15 9 8	8 13 8	Printing and Office Expenses.
3 0 7½	–	–	2 10 0	0 13 0	Travelling and Police Charges.
37 9 5½	16 6 6	10 10 0	35 6 9	15 10 2	Medical Expenses, Funerals, &c.
7 7 10½	6 10 2	7 18 0	23 7 10	5 10 6	Sundries, Rewards, &c.
738 9 8	898 15 8	884 16 1	1,484 14 3	1,319 11 7	Total Ordinary Charges.
					Extra Charges.
65 0 0	–	15 0 0	200 0 0	41 10 0	Rent of School Premises.
–	50 0 0	31 0 11	–	250 0 0	Interest.
12 0 0	21 10 0	5 0 0	10 10 0	18 5 0	Disposal, Home.
–	3 10 0	–	3 15 0	–	Emigration and Passages.
–	–	–	–	–	Building and Land.
77 0 0	75 0 0	51 0 11	214 5 0	309 15 0	Total Extra Charges.
800 9 8	974 15 8	915 17 0	1,699 3 3	1,629 6 7	Total Expenditure.
					INDUSTRIAL DEPARTMENT.
78 8 4	53 0 6	14 10 2	258 14 9	160 18 9	Profit (including Stock on hand and Bills).
–	–	–	–	–	Loss, do.

13.—Industrial Schools.—Return of Receipts &c,

Receipts and Expenditure.	St. Aloysius', Clonakilty, Girls.	St. Coleman's, Queenstown, Girls.	Our Lady of Mercy, Kinsale, Girls.	Baltimore, Upton, Co. Cork, Boys.	St. John's Home, Union Quay, Girls
	11.	12.	13.	14.	15.
Average Number of Children paid for by Treasury.	150	48	150	101	16
Average Number of Children under 6 years of age, and not yet paid for by Treasury.	1	–	*4	–	–
Average Number of Children in excess of limit, and not yet paid for by Treasury.	6	–	*4	2	–
Average Number of Voluntary Inmates.	7	*20	–	–	18
Receipts.	£ s. d.	£ s. d.	£ s. d.	£ s. d.	£ s. d.
Treasury Allowances,	1,694 13 8	599 12 3	1,953 6 9	2,258 19 8	218 1 0
Subscriptions, Legacies, Donations, &c.	–	–	–	–	7 0 6
Payments from County and Borough Rates.	584 10 8	177 2 8	682 16 2	497 1 6	68 9 2
Payments for Voluntary Inmates.	80 0 0	–	–	10 0 0	124 7 6
Hire of Labour,	28 0 0	–	–	–	–
Sundries,	–	–	–	8 18 2	44 0 6
Total Receipts,	2,385 5 11	775 15 11	2,636 2 11	2,774 19 4	457 18 0
Expenditure.					
Ordinary Charges.					
Officers' Pay (Salaries & House Wages).	86 0 0	71 5 6	83 10 0	602 11 6	17 10 0
Officers' Rations,	128 0 0	20 0 0	144 0 0	266 0 0	26 0 0
Food for Inmates,	1,472 2 8	400 12 7	1,238 16 0	951 7 8	216 17 [illegible]
Clothing of Inmates,	289 6 4	116 10 9	409 8 4	311 2 8	76 6 3
Washing, Fuel, and Light,	188 5 11	40 8 8	175 14 10	265 11 8	67 11 9
Repairs, Rates, and Taxes,	37 7 0	35 0 8	90 6 10	79 18 8	25 15 10
Furniture and House Sundries,	26 0 0	7 9 8	40 17 2	298 1 7	8 8 7
Printing and Office Expenses,	10 9 8	4 0 8	20 0 8	30 18 11	0 4 9
Travelling and Police Charges,	7 3 10	1 18 8	–	18 6 6	–
Medical Expenses, Funerals, &c.,	22 4 0	22 5 0	80 12 10	40 8 9	8 5 8
Sundries, Rewards, &c.,	15 0 0	11 7 8	18 4 2	62 8 8	21 8 4
Total Ordinary Charges,	2,218 10 0	740 5 8	2,340 10 8	2,078 9 0	481 8 10
Extra Charges.					
Rent of School Premises,	–	90 0 0	24 0 0	–	30 0 0
Interest,	270 0 0	–	300 0 0	218 6 4	–
Disposal, Home,	30 0 2	–	74 13 0	7 10 0	–
" Emigration and Passages	3 10 0	–	–	2 18 0	8 0 6
Building and Land,	115 9 11	125 0 0	–	298 4 6	–
Total Extra Charges,	422 0 6	215 0 0	398 13 0	521 10 10	38 0 5
Total Expenditure,	2,641 11 2	955 5 8	2,739 3 5	2,599 19 10	489 8 [illegible]
Industrial Department.					
Profit (including Stock on hand and Bills).	270 10 4	75 0 0	216 18 7	868 13 4	67 0 5
Loss, do.,	–	–	–	–	–

* Cost of maintenance not included in expenditure

and EXPENDITURE for, the Year 1880—*continued.*

[illegible], Cork. Boys. 16.	Mallow. Girls. 17.	Passage West. Boys. 18.	Baltimore, Co. Cork. Boys. 19.	St. Finbar's, Cork. Girls. 20.	RECEIPTS AND EXPENDITURE.
51	60	83	106	183	Average Number of Children paid for by Treasury.
1	*1	3	-	10	Average Number of Children under 6 years of age, and not yet paid for by Treasury.
-	*9	2	2	6	Average Number of Children in excess of Staff, and not yet paid for by Treasury.
8	*5	11	-	3	Average Number of Voluntary Inmates.
					RECEIPTS.
£ s. d.	£ s. d.	£ s. d.	£ s. d.	£ s. d.	
640 6 [illegible]	782 8 [illegible]	415 15 8	1,280 3 [illegible]	1,718 10 [illegible]	Treasury Allowances.
545 15 0	..	800 0 0	45 17 [illegible]	-	Subscriptions, Legacies, Donations, &c.
185 0 0	248 17 8	123 0 10	405 18 1	470 18 2	Payments from County and Borough Rates.
-	-	130 0 [illegible]	-	51 0 0	Payments for Voluntary Inmates.
-	-	-	-	-	Hire of Labour.
-	-	-	-	769 15 0	Sundries.
1,371 10 [illegible]	1,031 0 8	869 [illegible] 1	1,787 15 10	2,811 3 [illegible]	Total Receipts.
					EXPENDITURE.
					Ordinary Charges.
181 10 [illegible]	40 0 [illegible]	40 0 0	280 6 3	378 0 [illegible]	Officers' Pay (Salaries & House Wages).
60 0 [illegible]	81 0 0	60 0 0	120 0 0	310 0 0	Officers' Rations.
457 11 [illegible]	409 15 3	840 0 0	623 12 [illegible]	1,104 10 [illegible]	Food for Inmates.
228 8 [illegible]	143 8 [illegible]	78 0 0	391 17 1[illegible]	283 0 10	Clothing of Inmates.
80 11 [illegible]	97 9 6	70 0 0	111 8 10	204 18 [illegible]	Washing, Fuel, and Light.
84 15 [illegible]	54 0 0	80 0 0	98 14 [illegible]	87 17 7	Repairs, Rates, and Taxes.
89 17 0	104 4 1	85 0 0	172 14 [illegible]	167 0 [illegible]	Furniture and House Sundries.
4 7 4	20 10 0	15 0 0	40 11 11	11 14 10	Printing and Office Expenses.
7 18 4	3 10 0	1 0 0	85 18 4	0 11 [illegible]	Travelling and Police Charges.
8 8 1	23 18 3	5 10 0	44 19 [illegible]	83 0 3	Medical Expenses, Funerals, &c.
31 5 4	18 0 0	15 0 0	-	31 0 [illegible]	Sundries, Rewards, &c.
1,101 4 11	851 10 4	706 10 0	1,686 5 0	2,349 14 [illegible]	Total Ordinary Charges.
					Extra Charges.
125 [illegible] 0	-	25 0 0	21 8 0	67 10 0	Rent of School Premises.
14 7 11	100 0 0	75 0 0	9 4 8	-	Interest.
105 7 10	85 0 0	15 10 0	-	75 10 0	Disposal. Hotel.
-	-	-	-	37 0 0	" Emigration and Passages.
-	-	75 0 0	623 18 5	80 [illegible] 0	Building and Land.
245 [illegible] 9	185 0 0	190 10 0	654 5 1	270 [illegible] [illegible]	Total Extra Charges.
1,346 0 8	1,036 15 4	896 0 0	2,340 11 1	2,619 19 2	Total Expenditure.
					INDUSTRIAL DEPARTMENT.
125 19 0	10 15 11	8 0 0	578 8 7	180 15 4	Profit (including Stock on hand and Bills).
-	-	-	-	-	Loss, do.

* Cost of maintenance not included in expenditure.

14.—Industrial Schools.—Return of Receipts in,

Receipts and Expenditure.	Greenmount, Cork. Boys. 21.	St. Nicholas', Cove-street, Cork. Boys. 22.	Training Home, Union-quay, Cork. Girls. 23.	Artane, Co. Dublin. Boys. 24.	Booterstown, Co. Dublin. Girls. 25.
Average Number of Children paid for by Treasury.	187	68	88	793	164
Average Number of Children under 6 years of age, and not yet paid for by Treasury.	-	-	1	1	-
Average Number of Children in excess of limit, and not yet paid for by Treasury.	-	-	-	6	4
Average Number of Voluntary Inmates.	-	1	-	6	-
Receipts.	£ s. d.	£ s. d.	£ s. d.	£ s. d.	£ s. d.
Treasury Allowances,	2,498 10 9	908 14 6	497 4 0	10,880 0 4	1,786 16 8
Subscriptions, Legacies, Donations, &c.	67 10 0	140 10 2	10 12 5	1,287 17 2	103 0 0
Payments from County and Borough Rates.	867 17 7	288 13 0	143 18 3	4,604 14 10	655 5 8
Payments for Voluntary Inmates.	-	1 0 0	-	99 19 4	-
Hire of Labour,	-	4 5 0	-	-	-
Sundries,	-	12 6 6	17 14 2	53 19 2	80 6 8
Total Receipts,	3,370 18 4	1,355 11 2	668 4 3	16,896 10 11	2,651 5 4
Expenditure.					
Ordinary Charges.					
Officers' Pay (Salaries & House Wages).	539 0 0	240 0 0	25 5 0	2,290 1 0	98 0 0
Officers' Rations,	250 0 0	87 0 0	40 0 0	600 0 0	105 0 0
Food for Inmates,	1,278 8 4	483 7 10	303 7 8	6,825 7 4	1,280 6 8
Clothing of Inmates,	486 8 3	251 0 8	101 19 4	2,489 6 4	874 10 10
Washing, Fuel, and Light,	168 13 0	176 19 3	90 3 2	720 1 9	191 0 0
Repairs, Rates, and Taxes,	177 0 8	59 15 1	73 2 8	344 8 8	110 0 0
Furniture and House Sundries,	158 10 3	104 1 8	47 8 10	536 18 10	102 3 8
Printing and Office Expenses,	32 13 10	27 1 4	1 13 6	333 19 6	24 5 3
Travelling and Police Charges,	68 16 0	3 9 2	5 7 9	178 9 6	19 0 8
Medical Expenses, Funerals, &c.,	38 11 4	21 11 0	4 11 4	125 17 10	73 1 6
Sundries, Rewards, &c.,	68 17 0	24 10 6	20 7 6	398 18 8	80 9 1
Total Ordinary Charges,	3,440 8 4	1,516 10 11	712 8 0	14,628 17 11	2,449 10 6
Extra Charges.					
Rent of School Premises,	25 10 0	-	35 0 0	150 0 0	47 17 6
Interest,	228 10 0	-	-	1,796 2 4	-
Disposal, Home,	75 5 0	12 10 8	29 18 7	650 0 6	103 10 0
" Emigration and Passages,	-	-	-	20 0 0	-
Building and Land,	-	-	-	962 18 1	138 0 8
Total Extra Charges,	329 5 0	12 10 8	64 18 7	3,316 0 11	289 7 6
Total Expenditure,	3,769 13 4	1,529 1 7	777 17 0	17,944 18 10	2,737 17 11
Industrial Department.					
Profit (including Stock on hand and Bills).	857 18 6	227 10 8	118 5 7	1,442 0 10	169 14 3
Loss, &c.,	-	-	-	-	-

[illegible]turns for the Year 1890—*continued.*

[illegible] Industrial School, Boys.	St. Mary's, [illegible], Co. Dublin, Girls.	[illegible], Blackrock, Co. Dublin, Boys.	[illegible], Co. Dublin, Girls.	RECEIPTS AND EXPENDITURE.
21.	22.	23.	24.	
100	70	124	150	Average Number of Children paid for by Treasury.
–	1	–	–	Average Number of Children under 6 years of Age, and not yet paid for by Treasury.
–	–	–	1	Average Number of Children in excess of Limit, and not yet paid for by Treasury.
–	2	–	–	Average Number of Voluntary Inmates.
£ s. d.	£ s. d.	£ s. d.	£ s. d.	RECEIPTS.
305 8 10	915 0 0	1,596 17 0	1,955 7 0	Treasury Allowances.
–	–	61 19 0	–	Subscriptions, Legacies, Donations, &c.
588 0 11	341 4 0	654 11 0	741 13 0	Payments from County and Borough Rates.
–	–	–	–	Payments for Voluntary Inmates.
–	–	–	20 0 0	Hire of Labour.
–	–	11 13 [illegible]	–	Sundries.
[illegible]893 0 [illegible]	1,257 4 0	2,321 1 [illegible]	2,705 19 2	Total Receipts.
				EXPENDITURE.
				Ordinary Charges.
403 11 4	88 0 0	271 0 0	107 0 0	Officers' Pay (Salaries & Wages).
130 0 0	78 0 0	–	280 0 0	Officers' Rations.
318 0 0	586 15 0	830 19 2	1,540 0 0	Food for Inmates.
302 0 0	72 10 0	407 3 2	250 0 0	Clothing for Inmates.
108 0 0	60 0 0	145 5 4	200 0 0	Washing, Fuel, and Light.
0 0 0	104 15 0	97 7 11	180 0 0	Repairs, Rates, and Taxes.
54 4 0	80 0 0	101 17 5	130 0 0	Furniture and House Sundries.
24 0 0	6 10 0	46 3 0	30 0 0	Printing and Office Expenses.
20 0 0	8 17 0	3 3 10	–	Travelling and Police Charges.
24 3 10	11 9 10	53 14 10	46 0 0	Medical Expenses, Funerals, &c.
10 0 0	18 0 0	208 7 [illegible]	60 0 0	Sundries, Rewards, &c.
[illegible]950 8 [illegible]	1,188 17 10	2,217 17 10	2,903 0 0	Total Ordinary Charges.
				Extra Charges.
40 0 0	98 10 0	82 5 0	50 0 0	Rent of School Premises.
–	180 0 0	12 8 0	142 10 0	Interest.
38 0 0	20 0 0	114 4 1	70 0 0	Disposal, Home.
2 0 0	–	–	–	,, Emigration and Passage.
–	–	–	–	Building and Land.
68 0 0	303 10 0	158 18 0	263 10 0	Total Extra Charges.
[illegible]018 8 8	1,492 7 10	2,376 11 4	3,166 10 0	Total Expenditure.
				INDUSTRIAL DEPARTMENT.

14.—Industrial Schools.—Return of Receipts in,

Receipts and Expenditure.	[illegible]-street, Dublin. Girls. 31.	St. Bridget's, Loughrea. Girls. 32.	St. Joseph's, Ballinasloe. Girls. 33.	Clifden, Co. Galway. Girls. 34.	Letterfrack, Co. Galway. Boys. 35.
Average Number of Children paid for by Treasury.	48	119	60	80	169
Average Number of Children under 6 years of age, and not yet paid for by Treasury.	-	-	-	*4	-
Average Number of Children in excess of limit, and not yet paid for by Treasury.	-	-	10	-	-
Average Number of Voluntary Inmates.	-	*38	4	-	-
Receipts.	£ s. d.	£ s. d.	£ s. d.	£ s. d.	£ s. d.
Treasury Allowances,	868 10 9	1,440 5 8	783 8 8	1,041 1 9	1,949 4 9
Subscriptions, Legacies, Donations, &c.	23 17 0	-	-	-	-
Payments from County and Borough Rates.	287 4 7	574 2 2	356 8 0	423 14 7	624 14 8
Payments for Voluntary Inmates.	-	-	-	-	-
Hire of Labour,	-	-	-	-	-
Sundries,	1 3 4	-	-	-	-
Total Receipts,	981 4 8	2,014 7 8	1,188 6 8	1,463 16 4	2,576 19
Expenditure.					
Ordinary Charges.					
Officers' Pay (Salaries & House Wages).	98 18 0	112 0 0	60 0 0	129 0 0	53 14 4
Officers' Rations,	83 6 0	107 0 0	75 0 0	18 0 0	250 10 6
Food for Inmates,	282 19 6	680 0 0	501 10 6	648 11 4	1,460 14 9
Clothing of Inmates,	181 10 4	400 7 0	245 4 9	230 10 0	470 5 9
Washing, Fuel, and Light,	104 15 4	180 10 8	73 3 4	75 4 10	169 6 6
Repairs, Rates, and Taxes,	54 18 0	57 5 0	27 19 0	87 8 4	79 14 9
Furniture and House Sundries,	10 3 0	148 16 6	48 4 8	40 9 9	48 10 8
Printing and Office Expenses,	8 4 5	8 7 0	14 18 6	18 8 11	80 4 6
Travelling and Police Charges,	9 14 6	5 10 0	-	-	26 4 0
Medical Expenses, Funerals, &c.,	89 2 4	3 13 6	24 10 0	7 11 5	30 0 0
Sundries, Rewards, &c.,	48 13 9	42 6 0	16 10 6	15 0 0	97 10 6
Total Ordinary Charges,	940 4 5	1,700 12 8	1,097 0 6	1,209 18 5	2,520 16 0
Extra Charges.					
Rent of School Premises,	37 0 0	98 5 0	60 0 0	62 0 0	-
Interest,	-	40 5 0	200 0 0	25 0 0	120 0 0
Disposal, Home,	23 11 0	50 8 7	29 5 0	23 4 9	-
" Emigration and Passages,	-	88 0 0	5 5 0	6 0 0	-
Building and Land,	-	15 7 0	117 2 6	101 18 2	40 0 0
Total Extra Charges,	64 11 0	293 6 7	501 13 0	307 3 9	160 0 0
Total Expenditure,	994 15 5	1,988 19 3	1,598 18 6	1,516 15 7	2,680 16 0
Industrial Department.					
Profit (including Stock on hand and Bills).	105 8 8	9 19 6	120 13 5	63 0 0	58 18 10
Loss, do.,	-	-	-	-	-

* Cost of maintenance not included in expenditure.

and EXPENDITURE for the Year 1890—*continued.*

Oughterard, Co. Galway. Girls. 95.	St. Anne's, Galway. Girls. 87.	Salthill, Galway. Boys. 88.	St. Joseph's Home, Kilkenny. Boys. 89.	St. Joseph's, Tralee. Boys. 49.	RECEIPTS AND EXPENDITURE.
40	77	197	102	100	Average Number of Children paid for by Treasury.
–	1	–	–	–	Average Number of Children under 6 years of age, and not yet paid for by Treasury.
–	2	–	–	–	Average Number of Children in excess of limit, and not yet paid for by Treasury.
–	–	–	*6	–	Average number of Voluntary Inmates.
£ s. d.	£ s. d.	£ s. d.	£ s. d.	£ s. d.	RECEIPTS.
[illegible] 7 [illegible]	1,000 16 0	2,582 7 5	1,830 12 [illegible]	1,200 18 0	Treasury Allowances.
–	–	–	–	–	Subscriptions, Legacies, Donations, &c.
200 3 [illegible]	372 1 0	1,044 6 8	397 17 10	384 4 4	Payments from County and Borough Rates.
–	128 18 4	–	78 0 0	–	Payments for Voluntary Inmates.
–	–	–	–	–	Hire of Labour.
–	–	–	–	–	Sundries.
727 11 [illegible]	1,499 14 10	3,636 13 8	1,736 0 10	1,585 3 4	Total Receipts.
					EXPENDITURE.
					Ordinary Charges.
114 0 0	140 0 0	503 10 6	100 0 0	324 2 8	Officers' Pay (Salaries & House Wages).
90 0 0	45 0 0	279 8 [illegible]	68 0 0	190 0 0	Officers' Rations.
290 5 [illegible]	641 16 [illegible]	1,777 8 [illegible]	609 10 0	765 18 0	Food for Inmates.
68 15 [illegible]	250 5 4	960 5 6	180 0 0	284 8 4	Clothing of Inmates.
95 2 [illegible]	158 13 [illegible]	346 14 [illegible]	120 0 6	128 0 0	Washing, Fuel, and Light.
83 6 [illegible]	134 10 0	274 3 [illegible]	160 14 6	47 12 6	Repairs, Rates, and Taxes.
31 0 0	40 17 [illegible]	156 18 0	40 3 6	68 10 0	Furniture and House Sundries.
10 0 0	38 16 [illegible]	64 10 [illegible]	7 0 0	11 0 [illegible]	Printing and Office Expenses.
1 0 0	2 0 [illegible]	11 16 11	1 10 0	28 0 [illegible]	Travelling and Police Charges.
15 1 0	16 0 0	50 4 0	16 1 11	56 2 [illegible]	Medical Expenses, Funerals, &c.
–	10 6 0	20 2 8	20 0 1	25 1 0	Sundries, Rewards, &c.
743 14 [illegible]	1,486 3 4	3,938 18 [illegible]	1,160 4 0	1,942 7 10	Total Ordinary Charges.
					Extra Charges.
60 0 0	120 0 0	158 17 [illegible]	9 0 0	–	Rent of School Premises.
–	40 0 0	8[illegible]4 17 [illegible]	354 10 0	–	Interest.
18 0 0	30 0 0	68 13 [illegible]	18 10 4	12 10 0	Disposal, Home.
5 0 0	5 0 0	–	11 11 4	3 7 9	" Emigration and Passage.
–	–	5 13 [illegible]	–	–	Building and Land.
78 0 0	195 0 0	608 3 [illegible]	374 0 [illegible]	15 17 0	Total Extra Charges.
821 14 [illegible]	1,680 3 4	4,546 17 2	1,534 11 [illegible]	1,958 5 7	Total Expenditure.
					INDUSTRIAL DEPARTMENT.
91 5 11	160 8 6	153 6 4	74 18 5	284 9 5	Profit (including Stock on hand and Bills).
–	–	–	–	–	Loss, do.

* Cost of maintenance not included in expenditure.

14.—Industrial Schools.—Return of Receipts &c.

Receipts and Expenditure.	Pembroke Alms House, Tralee. Girls.	Kilkenny, Boys.	Kilkenny, Girls.	St. John's, Ballinasloe. Girls.	St. George's, Limerick. Girls.
	41.	42.	43.	44.	45.
Average Number of Children paid for by Treasury.	70	142	100	80	80
Average Number of Children under 6 years of age, and not yet paid for by Treasury.	*2	1	–	2	–
Average Number of Children in excess of limit, and not yet paid for by Treasury.	–	–	*5	1	16
Average Number of Voluntary Inmates.	*1	1	–	–	–
Receipts.	£ s. d.	£ s. d.	£ s. d.	£ s. d.	£ s. d.
Treasury Allowances,	690 11 8	2,122 15 0	1,310 2 9	1,038 14 8	1,282 17 6
Subscriptions, Legacies, Donations, &c.	–	83 10 11	25 3 6	–	–
Payments from County and Borough Rates.	186 2 6	765 3 6	341 7 11	388 15 7	508 8 5
Payments for Voluntary Inmates.	–	–	–	–	–
Hire of Labour,	–	–	–	–	–
Sundries,	–	–	–	–	–
Total Receipts,	1,095 14 3	2,967 9 5	1,676 13 2	1,427 10 3	1,846 0 11
Expenditure.					
Ordinary Charges.					
Officers' Pay (Salaries & House Wages).	66 0 0	198 0 0	140 0 0	92 10 0	180 0 0
Officers' Rations,	65 0 0	300 0 2	100 0 0	74 8 8	–
Food of Inmates,	504 10 6	1,612 11 3	1,152 15 6	706 5 11	632 10 10
Clothing of Inmates,	130 10 6	358 4 6	236 11 6	190 11 7	144 14 6
Washing, Fuel, and Light,	65 19 3	270 11 3	280 12 7	150 15 6	61 3 11
Repairs, Rates, and Taxes,	45 13 5	11 1 6	97 7 6	42 4 8	187 10 11
Furniture and House Sundries,	22 13 5	178 13 7	67 2 10	63 15 6	70 17 10
Printing and Office Expenses,	10 5 8	24 5 11	30 18 11	26 16 1	9 11 2
Travelling and Police Charges,	–	84 7 8	2 3 8	6 14 8	–
Medical Expenses, Funerals, &c.	25 10 0	62 16 4	15 2 8	28 10 0	18 18 1
Sundries, Rewards, &c.,	8 4 6	78 19 8	5 6 0	89 8 5	20 2 9
Total Ordinary Charges,	1,017 8 9	3,059 10 4	2,109 14 6	1,412 11 8	1,186 16 6
Extra Charges.					
Rent of School Premises,	–	73 5 6	17 0 0	18 12 10	93 0 8
Interest,	–	200 0 0	350 0 0	48 0 0	281 18 6
Disposal, Home,	36 13 6	–	93 0 0	30 0 8	30 6 3
„ Emigration and Passages.	22 19 4	–	–	–	–
Building and Land,	–	588 11 2	500 0 0	–	–
Total Extra Charges,	81 12 10	861 16 8	[illegible] 0 0	96 17 8	405 5 6
Total Expenditure,	[illegible]	[illegible]	3,0[illegible] 14 6	1,509 8 10	[illegible]
Industrial Department.					
Profit (including Stock on hand and Bills).	41 17 1	76 11 5	383 6 4	174 11 6	60 0 2
Loss, do.,	–	–	–	–	–

* Cost of maintenance not included in expenditure.

and Expenditure for, the Year 1890—*continued.*

St. Vincent's, Limerick. Girls.	[illegible], Boys.	Our Lady of [illegible], [illegible]. Girls.	House of Charity, [illegible]. Boys.	[illegible], Girls.	Receipts and Expenditure.
49.	51.	48.	49.	50.	
100	149	148	93	80	Average Number of Children paid for by Treasury.
*4	–	1	2	*6	Average Number of Children under 6 years of age, and not yet paid for by Treasury.
*15	–	7	9	*4	Average Number of Children in excess of limit, and not yet paid for by Treasury.
*26	*3	*9	2	*22	Average Number of Voluntary Inmates.
£ s. d.	£ s. d.	£ s. d.	£ s. d.	£ s. d.	**Receipts.**
1,694 18 3	1,033 2 0	1,688 7 6	1,306 1 8	1,049 17 6	Treasury Allowances.
–	16 3 9	–	–	–	Subscriptions, Legacies, Donations, &c.
437 8 4	775 14 8	784 18 0	583 17 11	490 9 6	Payments from County and Borough Rates.
–	32 2 6	–	100 0 0	–	Payments for Voluntary Inmates.
–	–	–	–	–	Hire of Labour.
–	33 11 6	–	–	–	Sundries.
2,132 16 7	2,760 18 6	2,423 1 8	1,847 18 11	1,543 6 4	Total Receipts.
					Expenditure.
					Ordinary Charges.
70 0 0	100 0 0	–	186 0 0	90 0 0	Officers' Pay (Salaries & House Wages).
181 18 4	176 14 0	260 0 0	107 0 0	150 0 0	Officers' Rations.
1,006 6 0	1,123 3 5	1,040 0 0	690 16 0	672 13 1	Food of Inmates.
309 5 6	388 15 11	835 7 11	290 17 6	189 0 0	Clothing of Inmates.
312 7 2	193 6 6	346 10 6	70 12 6	194 0 0	Washing, Fuel, and Light.
140 10 8	97 1 8	93 7 6	201 6 8	96 5 6	Repairs, Rates, and Taxes.
69 3 8	49 11 2	331 11 8	125 2 6	176 8 6	Furniture and House Sundries.
8 0 6	33 12 1	25 10 0	22 10 6	11 15 6	Printing and Office Expenses.
3 12 [illegible]	10 16 0	–	18 14 0	3 15 0	Travelling and Police Charges.
60 6 11	51 16 8	45 9 11	42 3 8	18 10 0	Medical Expenses, Funerals, &c.
62 0 0	51 8 8	46 0 0	11 0 [illegible]	20 0 4	Sundries, Rewards, &c.
2,217 6 0	2,523 6 2	2,988 17 8	1,882 17 1	1,606 13 8	Total Ordinary Charges.
					Extra Charges.
60 0 0	58 6 8	30 0 0	14 0 0	81 15 9	Rent of School Premises.
–	100 0 8	–	50 0 0	–	Interest.
168 0 0	20 13 0	77 6 2	–	45 0 0	Disposal, Home.
–	3 3 6	33 0 0	–	–	" Emigration and Passages.
115 6 10	–	–	–	47 5 0	Building and Land.
343 6 10	185 3 8	129 6 2	64 0 0	121 0 2	Total Extra Charges.
2,560 12 10	2,737 9 8	3,118 3 8	1,947 17 1	1,827 10 11	Total Expenditure.
					Industrial Department.
630 18 8	150 13 11	–	2 6 6	78 10 0	Profit (including Stock on hand and Bills).
–	–	16 4 11	–	–	Loss, do.

* Cost of maintenance not included in expenditure.

14.—Industrial Schools.—Return of Receipts in,

Receipts and Expenditure.	St. Columba's, Westport. Girls. 51.	Ballaghaderreen. Girls. 52.	St. Martha's, Monaghan. Girls. 53.	St. Monica's, Ramsgrange. Girls. 54.	Summerhill, Athlone. Girls. 55.
Average Number of Children paid for by Treasury.	105	75	87	44	138
Average Number of Children under 6 years of age, and not yet paid for by Treasury.	–	5	3	–	3
Average Number of Children in excess of limit, and not yet paid for by Treasury.	*2	3	4	–	14
Average Number of Voluntary Inmates.	*2	12	–	53	21
Receipts.	£ s. d.	£ s. d.	£ s. d.	£ s. d.	£ s. d.
Treasury Allowances,	1,468 12 8	977 14 6	873 8 1	672 8 4	1,732 15 [illegible]
Subscriptions, Legacies, Donations, &c.	–	53 0 1	–	–	110 6 [illegible]
Payments from County and Borough Rates.	587 1 5	374 12 8	585 8 0	205 1 4	762 5 [illegible]
Payments for Voluntary Inmates.	–	240 0 0	–	208 8 4	292 15 [illegible]
Hire of Labour,	–	–	–	–	–
Sundries,	–	–	–	–	50 8 [illegible]
Total Receipts,	1,318 14 0	1,076 0 8	1,458 11 1	1,088 18 1	2,960 4 [illegible]
Expenditure.					
Ordinary Charges.					
Officers' Pay (Salaries & House Wages).	50 0 0	94 4 4	170 0 0	106 0 0	348 10 [illegible]
Officers' Rations,	60 0 0	216 0 0	–	50 0 0	82 5 [illegible]
Food for Inmates,	801 19 11	786 16 7	650 12 0	688 9 2	1,321 10 [illegible]
Clothing of Inmates,	307 2 0	168 14 4	372 16 4	128 0 0	611 10 [illegible]
Washing, Fuel, and Light,	301 17 1	144 8 1	120 0 0	144 16 3	486 6 [illegible]
Repairs, Rates, and Taxes,	200 0 0	110 3 3	80 10 0	195 19 4	314 17 [illegible]
Furniture and House Sundries,	284 12 0	83 10 7	38 0 0	85 19 6	209 11 [illegible]
Printing and Office Expenses,	5 0 0	10 6 8	6 0 0	28 12 1	46 6 [illegible]
Travelling and Police Charges,	–	5 6 2	–	–	18 18 [illegible]
Medical Expenses, Funerals, &c.,	20 10 0	68 1 6	13 7 0	26 12 4	29 18 [illegible]
Sundries, Rewards, &c.,	–	49 17 4	14 10 0	27 10 2	18 5 [illegible]
Total Ordinary Charges,	2,021 0 0	1,480 1 2	1,260 17 10	1,432 7 1	3,066 14 [illegible]
Extra Charges.					
Rent of School Premises,	–	–	15 0 0	50 0 0	250 0 [illegible]
Interest,	210 0 0	825 0 0	48 0 0	–	–
Disposal, Home,	50 0 0	–	30 10 0	–	–
" Emigration and Passages,	10 0 0	–	–	16 2 2	–
Building and Land,	–	–	–	–	–
Total Extra Charges,	278 0 0	825 0 0	93 10 0	66 2 2	250 0 [illegible]
Total Expenditure,	2,297 0 0	1,805 1 2	1,352 7 10	1,498 9 10	3,286 14 [illegible]
Industrial Department.					
Profit (including Stock on hand and Bills).	370 0 0	120 0 0	95 7 8	460 7 8	424 6 2
Loss, do.,	–	–	–	–	–

* Cost of maintenance not included in expenditure.

and EXPENDITURE for the Year 1890—*continued.*

[illegible] Abbey, Tobercurry. Girls. 58.	St. Laurence, Sligo. Girls. 57.	[illegible] Boys. 58.	St. Augustine's, Templemore. Girls. 23.	St. Francis, Cashel. Girls. 60.	RECEIPTS AND EXPENDITURE.
50	180	150	60	100	Average Number of Children paid for by Treasury.
–	–	–	–	–	Average Number of Children under 6 years of age, and not yet paid for by Treasury.
5	–	5	6	–	Average Number of Children in excess of limit, and not yet paid for by Treasury.
–	85	[illegible]	[illegible]	–	Average Number of Voluntary Inmates.
£ s. d.	£ s. d.	£ s. d.	£ s. d.	£ s. d.	RECEIPTS.
551 11 9	1,564 0 0	1,342 10 0	735 0 3	1,421 14 0	Treasury Allowances.
20 0 0	–	267 10 0	12 0 0	–	Subscriptions, Legacies, Donations, &c.
376 18 7	600 13 8	338 14 0	348 15 2	470 0 5	Payments from County and Borough Rates.
–	573 1 7	10 0 0	–	–	Payments for Voluntary Inmates.
–	–	–	–	–	Hire of Labour.
–	–	83 2 0	–	–	Sundries.

14.—Industrial Schools.—Return of Receipts in

Receipts and Expenditure.	St. Louis, [illegible]. Girls.	Tipperary. Girls.	St. Catherine's, [illegible]. Girls.	Cappoquin, Waterford. Boys.	St. Dominick's, Waterford. Girls.
	61.	62.	63.	64.	65.
Average Number of Children paid for by Treasury.	40	64	100	80	120
Average Number of Children under 6 years of age, and not yet paid for by Treasury.	-	*4	-	1	6
Average number of Children in excess of limit, and not yet paid for by Treasury.	-	*11	3	-	13
Average Number of Voluntary Inmates.	-	*18	*8	4	9
Receipts.	£ s. d.	£ s. d.	£ s. d.	£ s. d.	£ s. d.
Treasury Allowances,	536 1 0	834 0 0	1,303 10 0	669 13 6	1,564 6 0
Subscriptions, Legacies, Donations, &c.	-	-	-	81 17 6	6 10 0
Payments from County and Borough Rates.	196 19 1	175 14 4	500 7 2	277 0 0	357 10 6
Payments for Voluntary Inmates.	-	405 3 0	30 0 0	29 0 0	-
Hire of Labour,	-	-	6 0 0	-	-
Sundries,	-	-	-	-	-
Total Receipts,	733 0 1	1,416 8 4	1,840 8 11	1,061 8 6	1,928 6 6
Expenditure.					
Ordinary Charges.					
Officers' Pay (Salaries & House Wages).	68 0 0	84 5 0	6 0 0	163 0 0	140 0 0
Officers' Rations,	65 0 0	100 13 10	1,118 0 0	107 0 0	152 8 4
Food for Inmates,	206 10 6	318 6 10½	65 0 0	487 17 1	1,180 18 6
Clothing of Inmates,	148 13 0	200 0 0	163 4 0	194 0 2	603 7 5
Washing, Fuel, and Light,	109 18 3	116 8 10½	118 18 6	123 11 10	218 8 8
Repairs, Rent, and Taxes,	23 0 0	84 18 4½	149 8 8	25 4 1	194 2 1
Furniture and House Sundries,	16 10 0	19 10 1½	81 10 10	60 13 5	107 8 6
Printing and Office Expenses,	11 0 0	9 0 9	7 10 0	0 16 4	78 4 9
Travelling and Police Charges,	-	-	-	1 18 11	9 9 4
Medical Expenses, Funerals, &c.,	13 10 0	8 5 4½	47 10 0	23 9 6	73 8 0
Sundries, Rewards, &c.,	12 0 0	20 1 5½	31 10 0	10 19 8	8 13 8
Total Ordinary Charges,	770 17 9	1,109 11 1	1,775 5 1	1,087 8 6	2,850 4 6
Extra Charges.					
Rent of School Premises,	-	91 1 0	-	80 0 0	100 0 0
Interest,	15 0 0	215 19 2	142 10 0	40 0 0	180 0 0
Dispensal, Home.	38 10 0	87 4 11	66 0 0	-	23 0 0
Emigration and Passages,	-	-	-	-	18 0 6
Building and Land,	-	-	-	280 10 4	-
Total Extra Charges,	53 10 0	268 18 1	208 10 0	840 10 4	828 0 0
Total Expenditure,	583 7 9	1,378 9 2	1,068 18 1	1,877 18 8	3,678 4 6
Industrial Department.					
Profit (including Stock on hand and Bills).	63 7 7	406 8 0	67 15 2	19 18 7	160 8 1
Loss, do.,	-	-	-	-	-

* Cost of maintenance not included in expenditure.

and EXPENDITURE for, the Year 1890—*continued.*

Mount Carmel, Moate. Girls. 66.	St. Aidan's, New Ross. Girls. 67.	St. Michael's, Wexford. Girls. 68.	Marsh, Bray. Girls. 69.	St. Kyran's, Rathdrum, Co. Wicklow. Boys. 70.	RECEIPTS AND EXPENDITURE.
63	70	105	41	50	Average Number of Children paid for by Treasury.
-	-	-	-	-	Average Number of Children under 6 years of age, and not yet paid for by Treasury.
-	5	-	-	7	Average Number of Children in excess of limit, and not yet paid for by Treasury.
-	3	6	-	6	Average Number of Voluntary Inmates.
£ s. d.	£ s. d.	£ s. d.	£ s. d.	£ s. d.	RECEIPTS.
635 5 6	911 17 3	1,373 17 0	578 11 0	651 16 0	Treasury Allowances.
-	-	-	-	-	Subscriptions, Legacies, Donations, &c.
318 10 [illegible]	310 10 9	146 18 6	251 6 11	250 2 6	Payments from County and Borough Rates.
-	37 0 0	133 15 [illegible]	-	90 0 [illegible]	Payments from Voluntary Inmates.
-	-	-	-	-	Hire of Labour.
11 16 6	-	-	0 8 0	-	Sundries.
910 13 [illegible]	1,258 8 0	1,653 8 6	760 7 11	991 18 6	Total Receipts.
					EXPENDITURE.
					Ordinary Charges.
117 0 6	128 0 0	83 0 0	187 8 7	276 0 [illegible]	Officers' Pay (Salaries & House Wages).
60 0 6	-	135 0 0	-	65 0 0	Officers' Rations.
373 13 6	674 6 7	939 18 [illegible]	386 7 [illegible]	464 13 4	Food for Inmates.
133 10 0	180 7 10	677 8 1	66 18 [illegible]	100 4 6	Clothing of Inmates.
83 10 0	89 10 0	170 4 7	130 5 6	98 6 6	Washing, Fuel, and Light.
16 0 0	84 11 1	125 0 5	12 11 6	25 15 6	Repairs, Rates, and Taxes.
86 0 0	90 19 1	98 16 11	13 5 11	90 10 0	Furniture and House Sundries.
4 0 0	18 10 8	4 14 4	18 0 7	10 8 2	Printing and Office Expenses.
-	-	9 10 1	11 13 6	10 19 3	Travelling and Police Charges.
10 0 0	32 16 0	41 16 11	4 15 1	64 0 0	Medical Expenses, Funerals, &c.
6 0 0	8 8 8	47 11 0	8 5 0	10 18 0	Sundries, Rewards, &c.
888 13 0	1,108 11 6	2,031 18 8	681 6 [illegible]	1,162 1 [illegible]	Total Ordinary Charges.
					Extra Charges.
91 0 0	80 0 0	8 0 0	-	-	Rent of School Premises.
100 0 0	217 8 0	93 4 0	200 0 0	22 10 0	Interest.
10 0 0	54 17 8	41 14 8	-	-	Disposal, Home.
-	-	-	37 14 8	-	" Emigration and Passage.
10 0 0	-	675 7 11	-	100 0 0	Building and Land.
211 0 0	302 0 8	817 6 7	237 14 [illegible]	122 10 0	Total Extra Charges.
1,047 13 0	1,404 11 11	2,849 5 5	639 0 1[illegible]	1,284 11 [illegible]	Total Expenditure.
					INDUSTRIAL DEPARTMENT.
60 10 0	59 3 8	114 16 [illegible]	117 13 [illegible]	-	Profit (including Stock on hand and Bills).
-	-	-	-	6 16 [illegible]	Loss, do.

15.—INDUSTRIAL SCHOOLS.—SUMMARY of ACCOUNTS of RECEIPTS

INDUSTRIAL SCHOOLS.	Total Number of Children whose Maintenance is included in Expenditure.	Total Cost of Maintenance and Management.	Add Rent and Interest.
		£ s. d.	£ s. d.
1. Grampian,	843	4,789 10 9	—
2. Fox Lodge,	105	1,685 17 6	9 9 6
3. Hampton House,	163	1,474 9 7	141 13 6
4. St. Patrick's, Milltown,	101	2,697 15 6	98 0 0
5. St. Patrick's, Crumlin Road,	113	2,899 1 6	150 0 0
6. Shamrock Lodge,	40	773 0 8	60 0 0
7. Middletown,	54	899 15 7	50 0 0
8. Lurgan,	63	894 16 1	48 6 11
9. St. Joseph's, Cavan,	86	1,484 18 3	380 0 0
10. Ennis,	87	1,910 11 7	291 10 0
11. St. Aloysius, Clonakilty,	114	2,012 18 6	270 0 0
12. St. Coleman's, Queenstown,	45	748 5 6	60 0 0
13. Our Lady of Mercy, Kinsale,	140	2,340 18 9	834 0 0
14. Dannefort, Upton,	193	6,078 6 6	710 4 4
15. St. John's Home,	79	461 2 10	80 0 0
16. Marble Hill, Cork,	66	1,101 4 11	130 18 11
17. Mallow,	60	681 15 4	100 0 0
18. Passage West,	45	705 19 0	100 0 0
19. Baltimore,	196	1,833 5 0	30 13 0
20. St. Finbar's, Cork,	149	2,340 14 8	87 10 0
21. Greenmount, Cork,	197	6,460 8 4	256 0 0
22. St. Nicholas, Cove-street, Cork,	68	1,516 10 11	—
23. Training Home,	36	718 0 9	80 0 0
24. Artane,	809	14,928 17 11	1,960 7 4
25. Booterstown,	186	2,440 10 3	67 17 1
26. Golden Bridge,	188	2,869 14 4	769 18 11
27. Kilmore,	100	1,850 3 5	48 0 0
28. St. Mary's, Lakelands,	73	1,163 17 10	270 10 0
29. Meath, co. Dublin,	134	2,217 17 10	44 0 0
30. Merrion,	151	2,834 0 0	198 10 1
31. Heytesbury-street, Dublin,	43	868 4 0	37 0 0
32. St. Bridget's, Loughrea,	119	1,706 19 6	103 10 0
33. St. Joseph's, Ballinasloe,	65	1,047 0 0	444 0 0
34. Clifden,	86	1,898 13 5	85 0 0
35. Letterfrack,	49	2,069 10 0	189 0 0
36. Oughterard,	49	743 14 6	65 0 0
37. St. Anne's, Galway,	60	1,465 3 4	180 0 0
38. Salt Hill, Galway,	187	6,016 12 6	542 14 0
39. St. Joseph's, Killarney,	107	1,480 4 6	848 16 0
40. St. Joseph's, Tralee,	194	1,042 7 10	—

and Expenditure during the year ending 31st December, 1890.

Add Expenses of Disposal.	Deduct Industrial Profit.	Add Industrial Loss.	Net Cost per Head with these additions or deductions.	Industrial School.
£ s. d.	£ s. d.	£ s. d.	£ s. d.	
152 15 2	—	—	19 17 3	Grampian.
—	—	34 5 9	16 4 1	Fox Lodge.
80 0 0	148 18 10	—	14 5 8	Hampton House.
47 5 9	81 14 5	—	19 9 3	St. Patrick's, Milltown.
115 16 3	—	9 14 7	21 15 11	St. Patrick's, Crumlin Road.
17 0 0	73 4 3	—	15 4 0	Shamrock Lodge.
35 0 0	63 0 0	—	16 17 4	Middletown.
5 0 0	14 10 2	—	17 9 1	Lurgan.
11 4 0	213 14 3	—	16 14 11	St. Joseph's, Cavan.
15 5 0	160 11 0	—	17 15 2	Ennis.
38 10 4	770 10 4	—	16 12 0	St. Aloysius, Clonakilty.
—	16 9 0	—	15 4 6	St. Coleman's, Queenstown.
54 16 9	716 13 7	—	15 15 3	Our Lady of Mercy, Kinsale.
10 0 8	387 18 4	—	16 2 11	Dunmanway, Upton.
0 9 3	67 0 5	—	19 4 9	St. John's Home.
133 7 10	122 19 6	—	20 7 9	Marble Hill, Cork.
31 6 6	36 16 11	—	17 15 7	Mallow.
15 10 0	8 0 0	—	19 15 9	Passage West.
—	378 0 7	—	13 7 8	Baltimore.
102 10 0	109 10 4	—	15 13 9	St. Finbar's, Cork.
76 1 0	217 10 5	—	19 4 10	Greenmount, Cork.
17 10 5	327 10 6	—	14 17 3	St. Nicholas, Cove-street, Cork.
96 15 7	126 5 7	—	18 10 9	Training Home.
360 0 0	1,439 9 10	—	11 6 9	Artane.
137 10 0	160 16 3	—	17 14 11	Booterstown.
135 0 0	477 9 11	—	17 6 7	Golden Bridge.
90 0 0	193 17 8	—	19 9 3	Kilmore.
30 0 0	74 18 0	—	19 0 0	St. Mary's, Lakelands.
114 4 1	184 13 2	—	17 18 0	Meath, co. Dublin.
70 0 0	427 18 4	—	18 7 10	Merrion.
73 11 0	105 3 3	—	20 18 9	Heytesbury-street, Dublin.
63 0 7	9 11 0	—	17 3 9	St. Brigid's, Longford.
84 10 0	170 17 5	—	10 7 11	St. Joseph's, Ballinasloe.
20 4 0	16 0 0	—	16 17 11	Clifden.
—	84 19 10	—	16 11 0	Letterfrack.
36 0 0	81 8 11	—	18 5 1	Oughterard.
33 0 0	189 6 0	—	18 16 11	St. Anne's, Galway.
45 13 8	145 0 4	—	12 9 1	Salt Hill, „
30 10 8	71 16 0	—	17 5 0	St. Joseph's, Killarney.
15 17 0	304 3 5	—	19 14 9	St. Joseph's, Tralee.

15.—Industrial Schools.—Summary of Accounts of

Industrial School.	Total Number of Children whose Maintenance is included in Expenditure.	Total Cost of Maintenance and Management.	Add Rent and Interest.
		£ s. d.	£ s. d.
41. Pembroke Alms House, Tralee,	70	1,817 8 3	—
42. Kilkenny, Boys,	184	4,059 16 4	240 8 0
43. Do. Girls,	106	2,169 14 6	197 0 0
44. St. John's, Parsonstown,	83	1,413 11 8	69 10 [illegible]
45. St. George's, Limerick,	68	1,380 14 9	871 10 6
46. St. Vincent's, Limerick,	130	2,217 8 0	68 0 0
47. Limerick, Boys,	149	3,403 0 9	163 0 6
48. Our Lady of Succour, Newtownforbes,	163	2,688 17 9	39 0 0
49. House of Charity, Drogheda,	96	1,640 17 1	64 0 0
50. Dundalk,	60	1,646 10 6	31 13 9
51. St. Columba, Westport,	186	2,971 0 8	364 8 0
52. Ballaghaderreen,	85	1,486 1 3	120 0 0
53. St. Martha's, Monaghan,	76	1,536 17 10	64 0 0
54. St. Monica's, Roscommon,	77	1,433 7 1	64 0 0
55. Summerhill, Athlone,	171	2,805 14 4	150 0 0
56. Benada Abbey, Tubbercurry,	65	618 2 2	53 16 0
57. St. Laurence, Sligo,	168	2,686 17 8	713 12 9
58. Clonmel,	153	2,536 4 3	279 0 4
59. St. Augustine's, Templemore,	96	1,600 11 0	180 0 0
60. St. Francis, Cashel,	109	1,804 14 5	60 0 0
61. St. Louis, Thurles,	45	775 17 0	10 0 0
62. Tipperary,	84	1,198 11 11	136 13 8
63. St. Catherine's, Strabane,	103	1,778 8 1	148 16 0
64. Cappoquin,	50	1,037 8 4	66 8 0
65. St. Dominick's, Waterford,	148	2,500 4 0	120 0 0
66. Mount Carmel, Moate,	53	880 18 0	181 0 0
67. St. Aidan's, New Ross,	70	1,103 11 0	217 9 0
68. St. Michael's, Wexford,	119	2,031 10 0	109 4 0
69. Meath, Bray,	61	901 0 5	108 8 9
70. St. Kyran's, Rathdrum,	65	1,102 1 3	23 16 0

RECEIPTS and EXPENDITURE in 1890—*continued.*

Add Expenses of Disposal.	Deduct Industrial Profit.	Add Industrial Loss.	Net Cost per Head with these additions or deductions.	INDUSTRIAL SCHOOL.
£ s. d.	£ s. d.	£ s. d.	£ s. d.	
31 19 10	41 17 1	—	15 2 6	Pembroke Alms House, Tralee.
—	76 11 5	—	20 6 1	Kilkenny Boys.
23 8 6	263 6 4	—	21 15 8	Do. Girls.
28 3 4	174 11 5	—	16 1 7	St. John's, Parsonstown.
38 5 5	86 9 2	—	15 10 8	St. George's, Limerick.
150 8 5	428 10 5	—	18 16 2	St. Vincent's, Limerick.
37 14 6	108 12 11	—	17 1 11	Limerick, Boys.
40 6 8	—	15 4 11	24 9 11	Our Lady of Succour, Newtownforbes.
—	3 6 6	—	10 17 8	House of Charity, Drogheda.
42 8 8	76 18 5	—	20 5 9	Dundalk.
16 8 6	375 8 5	—	19 4 4	St. Columba's, Westport.
—	178 6 0	—	17 14 5	Ballaghaderreen.
65 18 6	95 7 8	—	16 14 8	St. Martha's, Monaghan.
16 3 9	460 7 5	—	15 5 7	St. Monica's, Roscommon.
—	474 6 2	—	17 5 6	Summerhill, Athlone.
—	88 6 0	—	16 11 1	Benada Abbey, Tubbercurry.
—	139 18 7	—	18 3 5	St. Laurence, Sligo.
78 17 8	27 15 2	—	20 4 3	Clonmel.
39 5 6	190 4 2	—	18 5 5	St. Augustine's, Templemore.
60 5 8	165 9 10	—	17 3 3	St. Francis, Cashel.
69 15 6	62 7 7	—	17 7 1	St. Louis, Thurles.
37 4 11	465 5 0	—	18 8 7	Tipperary.
64 6 5	57 15 7	—	15 5 7	St. Catherine's, Strabane.
—	19 10 7	—	16 4 10	Cappoquin.
90 1 5	144 5 1	—	17 10 8	St. Dominick, Waterford.
10 0 5	83 15 5	—	18 15 7	Mount Carmel, Moate.
84 17 6	69 3 8	—	19 1 8	St. Aidan's, New Ross.
41 16 3	114 16 2	—	16 4 6	St. Michael's, Wexford.
37 14 6	117 13 7	—	19 1 1	Meath, Bray.
—	—	8 18 3	16 15 3	St. Kyran's, Rathdrum.

18.—**Return giving (1st), the Population of each County and Town in Ireland as taken at Census, 1891; (2nd), the Amount paid by each County for Support of Children in Reformatory Schools during the past year (1890); (3rd), the Number of Children under Detention in Reformatory Schools from each County on 31st December, 1890.**

Counties and Towns.	Population.	Amount contributed in 1890.	No. of Children under Detention in Reformatory Schools from each County on 31st Dec., 1890.
		£ s. d.	
Antrim,	[illegible]	431 5 4	35
Armagh,	[illegible]	79 7 6	16
Carlow,	[illegible]	46 10 11	6
Cavan,	111,917	40 2 6	3
Clare,	[illegible]	[illegible]	8
Cork,	[illegible]	110 7 8	[illegible]
Cork City,	[illegible]	[illegible]	[illegible]
Donegal,	185,211	12 10 8	3
Down,	[illegible]	[illegible]	[illegible]
Dublin,	[illegible]	[illegible]	[illegible]
Dublin City,	[illegible]	[illegible]	[illegible]
Fermanagh,	[illegible]	[illegible]	4
Galway,	[illegible]	[illegible]	[illegible]
Galway Town,	[illegible]	[illegible]	[illegible]
Kerry,	[illegible]	[illegible]	10
Kildare,	[illegible]	[illegible]	[illegible]
Kilkenny,	[illegible]	[illegible]	2
Kilkenny City,	[illegible]	[illegible]	3
King's,	[illegible]	[illegible]	[illegible]
Leitrim,	[illegible]	19 7 1	4
Limerick,	[illegible]	[illegible]	4
Limerick City,	[illegible]	[illegible]	[illegible]
Londonderry,	[illegible]	[illegible]	[illegible]
Longford,	[illegible]	[illegible]	2
Louth,	[illegible]	[illegible]	[illegible]
Drogheda Town,	[illegible]	[illegible]	[illegible]
Mayo,	[illegible]	[illegible]	[illegible]
Meath,	[illegible]	[illegible]	4
Monaghan,	[illegible]	[illegible]	[illegible]
Queen's,	[illegible]	[illegible]	[illegible]
Roscommon,	[illegible]	[illegible]	[illegible]
Sligo,	[illegible]	[illegible]	[illegible]
Tipperary, N.R.,	[illegible]	[illegible]	[illegible]
Tipperary, S.R.,	[illegible]	[illegible]	[illegible]
Tyrone,	[illegible]	[illegible]	[illegible]
Waterford,	[illegible]	[illegible]	[illegible]
Waterford City,	[illegible]	[illegible]	[illegible]
Westmeath,	[illegible]	[illegible]	[illegible]
Wexford,	[illegible]	[illegible]	[illegible]
Wicklow,	[illegible]	[illegible]	[illegible]
Total,	[illegible]	[illegible]	[illegible]

19.—Return giving (1st), the Population of each County and Town in Ireland as taken at Census, 1891; (2nd), the amount paid by each County for Support of Children in Industrial Schools during the past year (1890); (3rd), the Number of Children under Detention in Industrial Schools from each County on 31st December, 1890.

Counties and Towns.	Population.	Amount contributed in 1890.	No. of Children under Detention in Industrial Schools from each County on 31st Dec., 1890.
		£ s. d.	
Antrim,	[illegible]	[illegible]	[illegible]
Armagh,	[illegible]	[illegible]	[illegible]
Carlow,	[illegible]	—	7
Cavan,	[illegible]	11 0 0	[illegible]
Clare,	[illegible]	[illegible]	[illegible]
Cork,	[illegible]	[illegible]	[illegible]
Cork City,	75,070	[illegible]	[illegible]
Donegal,	[illegible]	[illegible]	[illegible]
Down,	[illegible]	[illegible]	[illegible]
Dublin,	[illegible]	[illegible]	[illegible]
Dublin City,	[illegible]	[illegible]	[illegible]
Fermanagh,	[illegible]	114 [illegible]	[illegible]
Galway,	[illegible]	[illegible]	[illegible]
Galway Town,	[illegible]	[illegible]	[illegible]
Kerry,	[illegible]	[illegible]	[illegible]
Kildare,	[illegible]	[illegible]	[illegible]
Kilkenny,	[illegible]	[illegible]	[illegible]
Kilkenny City,	[illegible]	[illegible]	[illegible]
King's,	[illegible]	[illegible]	[illegible]
Leitrim,	[illegible]	[illegible]	[illegible]
Limerick,	[illegible]	[illegible]	[illegible]
Limerick City,	[illegible]	[illegible]	[illegible]
Londonderry,	[illegible]	[illegible]	[illegible]
Longford,	[illegible]	[illegible]	[illegible]
Louth,	[illegible]	[illegible]	[illegible]
Drogheda Town,	[illegible]	[illegible]	[illegible]
Mayo,	[illegible]	[illegible]	[illegible]
Meath,	[illegible]	[illegible]	[illegible]
Monaghan,	[illegible]	[illegible]	[illegible]
Queen's,	[illegible]	—	[illegible]
Roscommon,	[illegible]	[illegible]	[illegible]
Sligo,	[illegible]	[illegible]	[illegible]
Tipperary, N. R.,	[illegible]	—	[illegible]
Tipperary, S. R.,	[illegible]	[illegible]	[illegible]
Tyrone,	[illegible]	[illegible]	[illegible]
Waterford,	[illegible]	[illegible]	[illegible]
Waterford City,	[illegible]	[illegible]	[illegible]
Westmeath,	[illegible]	[illegible]	[illegible]
Wexford,	[illegible]	[illegible]	[illegible]
Wicklow,	[illegible]	[illegible]	[illegible]
	[illegible]	[illegible]	[illegible]

20.—RETURN showing the Rates paid by each County per Head per Week for Children in Industrial and Reformatory Schools during the Year ending 31st of December, 1890.

Grand Jury or Town Council.	Rates.		Observations.
	To Reformatories.	To Industrial Schools.	
Co. Antrim, . .	3s. 6d.	2s. 6d. and 2s.	2s. to Boys' Home, Colbey Bridge, and Cavan Industrial Schools; 2s. 6d. to all others.
„ Armagh, . .	3s. 6d.	2s. 6d.	—
„ Carlow, . .	3s. 6d.	Nil.	—
„ Cavan, . .	3s. 6d.	Nil.	—
„ Clare, . .	3s. 6d.	2s.	—
„ Cork, . .	3s. 6d.	2s. and 1s. 6d.	2s. to Baneshane, Upton, Greenmount, Mackle Hill and Rathmore, Passage West, and St. Nicholas, Clonakilty, Queenstown, Union Quay, and St. John's Home.
City of Cork (Corporation).	3s. 6d.	2s., 1s. 6d., and 1s.	2s. for boys, 1s. 6d. for girls in Cork schools; and 1s. for girls in schools outside the city.
Co. Donegal, .	3s. 6d.	2s. 6d., 2s., 1s. 6d.	2s. 6d. to Fox Lodge, Milltown, [illegible], and Drogheda; 2s. to [illegible], Monaghan, [illegible], and Middletown, and 1s. 6d. to [illegible].
„ Down, . .	3s. 6d.	2s. 6d. and 2s.	2s. 6d. to all Industrial Schools, except [illegible]-street, Training Home, Cork, and St. Joseph's, [illegible], which are 2s.
„ Dublin, . .	3s. 6d.	2s.	—
City of Dublin, .	3s. 6d.	2s.	Excepting one or two small schools, which are paid 1s. 6d.
Co. Fermanagh,	3s. 6d.	2s. 6d. and 2s.	2s. to St. Joseph's, Cavan; all others, 2s. 6d.
„ Galway, . .	3s. 6d.	2s.	—
Town of Galway, .	3s. 6d.	2s. 6d. and 2s.	Clifden, 2s. 6d.; all others 2s.
Co. Kerry, . .	3s. 6d. and 3s.	2s. 6d., 2s., and 1s.	3s. 6d. to St. Conleth's, Philipstown, Reformatory School, and 3s. to St. Joseph's, Limerick. Several Industrial schools are paid different rates.
„ Kildare, . .	3s. 6d.	2s. 6d.	—
„ Kilkenny, . .	3s. 6d.	2s. 6d. and 2s.	2s. to Training Home, Union-quay, Cork, St. Aidan's, New Ross, and St. Francis, Cashel, Industrial Schools. All others 2s. 6d.
City of Kilkenny, .	3s. 6d.	2s. 6d., 2s., 1s. 6d., and 1s.	2s. 6d. to Artane; 1s. 6d. each to St. Joseph's and St. Patrick's, Kilkenny, 2s. and 1s. to St. Joseph's, Clonmel, and 1s. to Baltimore.
Co. King's, . .	3s. 6d.	2s. 6d. and 2s.	2s. 6d. to Artane Industrial School; 2s. to all others.
„ Leitrim, . .	3s. 6d.	2s. 6d. and 2s.	2s. to Cavan Industrial School; 2s. 6d. to all others.
„ Limerick, . .	3s. 6d.	2s. 6d. and 2s.	2s. 6d. to Cappoquin, St. Francis, Cashel, Athlone and [illegible] Industrial Schools; all others 2s.
City of Limerick, .	3s.	2s.	Only one Reformatory School is contributed to, viz.:—St. Joseph's, Limerick.
Co. Londonderry, .	3s. 6d. and 3s.	2s. 6d. and 2s.	2s. 6d. for boys and 2s. for girls in both Reformatory and Industrial Schools.
„ Longford, . .	3s. 6d.	2s. 6d.	—

90.—Return showing the Rates paid by each County—*continued*.

Grand Jury or Town Council.	Rates.		Observations.
	To Reformatories.	To Industrial Schools.	
Co. Louth,	3s. 6d.	2s. 6d.	—
Town of Drogheda,	3s. 6d. and 2s.	2s. 6d. and 2s.	3s. 6d. for boys and 2s. for girls in both Reformatory and Industrial Schools.
Co. Mayo,	3s. 6d.	3s.	—
„ Meath,	3s. 6d.	2s. 6d. and 3s.	3s. to St. Aidan's, New Ross, Industrial School; 2s. 6d. to all others.
„ Monaghan,	3s. 6d.	3s. 6d. and 2s.	3s. to Middletown, [illegible]-street, and St. Joseph's, Cavan, Industrial School, and 2s. 6d. to all others.
„ Queen's,	3s. 6d. and 2s.	Nil.	3s. 6d. to Spark's Lake, Monaghan, Reformatory School, and 2s. each to St. Conleth's and St. Kevin's Reformatory Schools.
„ Roscommon,	3s. 6d. and 2s.	2s. 6d. and 2s.	3s. 6d. to High Park and Limerick Reformatories, and Artane and Tralee Industrial Schools, and 2s. to all others.
„ Sligo,	3s. 6d.	2s. 6d.	—
„ Tipperary, N.R.,	3s. 6d.	Nil.	—
„ Tipperary, S.R.,	3s. 6d.	2s. 6d.	The only children in Industrial Schools which are paid for are those in St. Joseph's, Clonmel, Industrial School.
„ Tyrone,	3s. 6d.	3s. 6d. and 2s.	3s. to St. Catherine's, Strabane, and [illegible], Cork, Industrial Schools; 2s. 6d. to all others. (b)
„ Waterford,	3s. 6d.	2s. 6d. and 2s.	3s. 6d. to Artane, and 2s. to all the others.
City of Waterford,	3s. 6d.	2s. 6d. and 2s.	2s. 6d. to Artane, Boys' Home, [illegible], [illegible], Upton, Greenmount, and Clonmel Industrial School, and 2s. to all the others.
Co. Westmeath,	—	—	—
„ Wexford,	3s. 6d. and 2s.	3s. 6d. and 2s. 6d.	3s. 6d. to Artane, Drogheda, Cappoquin, Clonmel, Letterfrack, St. Patrick's, Kilkenny, Dundalk, [illegible].
„ Wicklow,	3s.	2s.	—

21.—Showing the causes of Deaths of Children in Reformatory and Industrial Schools during the year ending 31st December, 1880.

Schools.	Lung Disease.	Brain Disease.	Heart Disease.	[illegible]	Fever.	Accidental Deaths.	Spinal and Hip Disease.	Other causes.	Total. Males.	Total. Females.	Total. Total.
Reformatories.											
Malone,	[illegible]	–	–	–	–	–	–	–	[illegible]	–	[illegible]
Glencree,	[illegible]	–	–	–	–	–	–	–	[illegible]	–	[illegible]
Philipstown,	[illegible]	1	–	–	–	–	–	–	[illegible]	–	[illegible]
Total Number of Deaths in Reformatory Schools,	[illegible]	1	–	–	–	–	–	–	[illegible]	–	[illegible]
Industrial Schools.											
[illegible],	[illegible]	[illegible]	–	[illegible]	–	[illegible]	–	[illegible]	[illegible]	–	[illegible]
[illegible] Lodge,	[illegible]	–	–	–	–	–	–	–	[illegible]	–	[illegible]
Hampton House,	[illegible]	–	1	–	–	–	–	–	[illegible]	[illegible]	[illegible]
St. Patrick's Male, Belfast,	[illegible]	–	–	[illegible]	–	–	–	–	[illegible]	–	[illegible]
St. Patrick's Female, Belfast,	[illegible]	1	–	–	–	–	–	–	–	[illegible]	[illegible]
Middletown,	[illegible]	[illegible]	–	–	–	–	–	–	–	[illegible]	[illegible]
Ennis,	[illegible]	–	–	–	–	–	–	–	–	[illegible]	[illegible]
Clonakilty,	[illegible]	–	–	–	–	–	–	–	–	[illegible]	[illegible]
Kinsale,	[illegible]	[illegible]	–	[illegible]	–	–	–	–	–	[illegible]	[illegible]
Upton,	[illegible]	[illegible]	–	–	–	–	–	–	[illegible]	–	[illegible]
Boys' Home, Marble-hill,	[illegible]	[illegible]	–	–	–	–	–	–	[illegible]	–	[illegible]
Mallow,	[illegible]	–	–	–	–	–	–	[illegible]	–	[illegible]	[illegible]
St. Finbarr's,	[illegible]	–	–	–	–	–	–	[illegible]	–	[illegible]	[illegible]
Greenmount,	[illegible]	[illegible]	–	–	1	–	–	–	[illegible]	–	[illegible]
Artane,	[illegible]	[illegible]	–	–	–	–	–	–	[illegible]	–	[illegible]
Booterstown,	[illegible]	[illegible]	–	–	–	–	–	–	–	[illegible]	[illegible]
Golden Bridge,	[illegible]	[illegible]	1	–	–	–	–	–	–	[illegible]	[illegible]
Blackrock, Co. Dublin,	[illegible]	[illegible]	–	–	–	–	–	–	–	[illegible]	[illegible]
Merrion,	[illegible]	–	[illegible]	–	–	–	–	–	–	[illegible]	[illegible]
Heytesbury-street,	[illegible]	–	–	[illegible]	–	–	–	–	–	[illegible]	[illegible]
Loughrea,	–	[illegible]	–	–	–	–	–	–	–	[illegible]	[illegible]
Ballinasloe,	[illegible]	–	–	–	–	–	–	–	–	[illegible]	[illegible]
Clifden, co. Galway,	[illegible]	–	–	–	–	–	–	–	–	[illegible]	[illegible]
St. Anne's, Galway,	[illegible]	–	–	–	–	–	–	–	–	[illegible]	[illegible]
Salthill, Galway,	[illegible]	–	–	–	–	–	–	[illegible]	[illegible]	–	[illegible]
St. Joseph's, Tralee,	[illegible]	–	–	–	–	–	–	–	[illegible]	–	[illegible]
St. Vincent's, Limerick,	[illegible]	–	–	–	–	–	–	–	[illegible]	[illegible]	[illegible]
[illegible],	[illegible]	1	–	–	1	–	–	–	[illegible]	–	[illegible]
[illegible],	[illegible]	–	–	–	–	–	–	–	–	[illegible]	[illegible]
Dundalk,	[illegible]	[illegible]	–	–	–	–	–	[illegible]	–	[illegible]	[illegible]
Westport,	[illegible]	1	–	–	–	–	–	[illegible]	–	[illegible]	[illegible]
Ballaghaderreen,	[illegible]	–	–	–	–	–	–	–	–	[illegible]	[illegible]
Monaghan,	[illegible]	–	–	–	–	–	–	–	–	[illegible]	[illegible]
Athlone,	[illegible]	–	–	–	–	–	1	–	–	[illegible]	[illegible]
Sligo,	[illegible]	–	–	–	–	–	–	–	–	[illegible]	[illegible]
Templemore,	–	–	–	–	–	–	–	–	–	[illegible]	[illegible]
[illegible],	–	–	–	–	–	–	–	[illegible]	–	[illegible]	[illegible]
Tipperary,	–	[illegible]	–	–	–	–	–	–	[illegible]	[illegible]	[illegible]
Cappoquin,	–	[illegible]	–	–	–	–	–	–	–	–	[illegible]
Waterford,	1	–	–	–	–	–	–	–	–	1	[illegible]
Mount Carmel, Moate,	–	–	–	–	–	–	–	[illegible]	–	1	[illegible]
St. Aidan's, New Ross,	–	–	1	–	–	–	–	–	–	1	[illegible]
St. Michael's, Wexford,	3	1	–	1	–	–	–	–	–	[illegible]	[illegible]
Total,	41	18	4	6	5	1	1	15	[illegible]	[illegible]	88

a. Measles; b. Dropsy. c. Convulsions. d. One from suppurative inflammation of the Ear, and one from Acute Laryngitis. e. Scrofula. f. Consumption. g. Liver Disease. h. [illegible].

22.—List of Thirty-two Industrial Departments (under the Act) in connexion with recognized National Schools on 31st December, 1890.

District.	Roll No.	School.	Name of Manager.	Address.	Date of last Report.	Date of Transmission of Copy to Reformatory Office.
[illegible]	[illegible]	Middletown,	Rev. C. M'Elroy, P.P.,	Middletown, Co. Armagh.	[illegible]	[illegible]
[illegible]	[illegible]	Ennis,	Rev. M. Carey, Adm.,	Ennis,	—*	—*
[illegible]	[illegible]	Mallow,	Very Rev. Canon Wigmore, P.P., V.G.	Mallow,	[illegible]	[illegible]
[illegible]	[illegible]	Clonakilty, St. Aloysius,	Mrs. M. G. O'Donoghue,	Convent, Clonakilty.	[illegible]	[illegible]
[illegible]	[illegible]	St. Coleman's, Queenstown.	Rev. John Barry, Adm.,	Queenstown,	[illegible]	[illegible]
[illegible]	[illegible]	St. Nicholas', Cork,	Rev. Canon Nicholson,	Cork,	[illegible]	[illegible]
[illegible]	[illegible]	Booterstown,	Very Rev. Canon Plunkett, P.P., V.G.	Booterstown,	[illegible]	[illegible]
[illegible]	[illegible]	St. Vincent's, Loughrea,	Mrs. Smyth,	Loughrea,	[illegible]	[illegible]
[illegible]	[illegible]	Oughterard,	Mrs. M. Turner,	Oughterard Convt.,	[illegible]	[illegible]
[illegible]	[illegible]	St. Anne's, Galway,	Mrs. M. Blake,	[illegible] Convt.,	[illegible]	[illegible]
[illegible]	[illegible]	Clifden, Galway,	Mrs. M. V. Ryan,	Clifden Convent,	[illegible]	[illegible]
[illegible]	[illegible]	St. Joseph's Home, Killarney.	Mrs. O'Farrell,	Convent of Mercy, Killarney.	[illegible]	[illegible]
[illegible]	[illegible]	Pembroke Alms, Tralee,	Mrs. O'[illegible],	Convent, Tralee,	[illegible]	[illegible]
[illegible]	[illegible]	St. Vincent's, Limerick,	Rev. J. O'Shea (?), Adm.,	St. Michael's, Limerick.	[illegible]	[illegible]
[illegible]	[illegible]	Our Lady of Succour, Newtownforbes.	Mrs. M. de S. Fallon,	Convent, Newtownforbes.	[illegible]	[illegible]
[illegible]	[illegible]	House of Charity, Drogheda.	Mrs. T. Austin,	Convent, Drogheda,	[illegible]	[illegible]
[illegible]	[illegible]	Dundalk,	Mrs. F. Duffy,	Convent, Dundalk,	[illegible]	[illegible]
[illegible]	[illegible]	St. Columba's, Westport,	Mrs. M. P. [illegible],	Convent, Westport,	[illegible]	[illegible]
[illegible]	446	St. Martha's, Monaghan.	Rev. D. M'[illegible], Adm.,	Monaghan,	[illegible]	[illegible]
[illegible]	[illegible]	St. Monica's, Roscommon.	Mrs. M. X. Hogan (?),	Convent, Roscommon.	[illegible]	[illegible]
[illegible]	[illegible]	St. Laurence's, Sligo,	Mrs. M. P. O'Beirne,	Convent, Sligo,	[illegible]	[illegible]
[illegible]	[illegible]	Benada Abbey, Tubbercurry.	Mrs. A. Connolly,	Benada Abbey, Tubbercurry.	[illegible]	[illegible]
[illegible]	[illegible]	St. Augustine's, Templemore.	Mrs. Walsh,	Convent, Templemore.	[illegible]	[illegible]
[illegible]	481	St. Francis, Cashel,	Mrs. Carroll,	Convent, Cashel,	[illegible]	[illegible]
[illegible]	[illegible]	St. Louis, Thurles,	Mrs. M. S. Hogan,	Convent, Thurles,	[illegible]	[illegible]
[illegible]	[illegible]	Tipperary,	Very Rev. Canon Cahill, P.P.	Tipperary,	[illegible]	[illegible]
[illegible]	[illegible]	St. Catherine's, Strabane,	Very Rev. R. O'[illegible], P.P., V.G.	Strabane,	[illegible]	[illegible]
[illegible]	[illegible]	Mount Carmel, Moate,	Mrs. M. [illegible],	Convent, Moate,	[illegible]	[illegible]
[illegible]	[illegible]	St. Michael's, Wexford,	Mrs. Johanna Ryan,	Convent of Mercy, Wexford.	[illegible]	[illegible]
[illegible]	[illegible]	Passage West, Cork,	Very Rev. P. L. Canon [illegible], P.P.	Passage West,	[illegible]	[illegible]
[illegible]	[illegible]	Ballinasloe,	Mrs. S. Burke,	Ballinasloe,	[illegible]	[illegible]
[illegible]	[illegible]	St. Joseph's, Athlone,	Mrs. M. J. Jones,	Summerhill, Athlone.	[illegible]	[illegible]

* No report yet received from Inspector.

† This Industrial School is not under the Board; but some of the children have attended the National School [illegible].

No. 18,823.

DUBLIN CASTLE,
16th July, 1891.

SIR,

I have to acknowledge the receipt of your letter of the 15th instant, forwarding, for submission to the Chief Secretary, your Annual Report on Reformatory and Industrial Schools in Ireland for the year 1890.

I am, Sir,
Your obedient servant,
W. S. B. KAYE.

The Inspector, Reformatory and
Industrial Schools.

DUBLIN: Printed for Her Majesty's Stationery Office,
By ALEX. THOM & Co. (Limited), 87, 88, & 89 Abbey-street.
The Queen's Printing Office.

www.ingramcontent.com/pod-product-compliance
Lightning Source LLC
Chambersburg PA
CBHW031449270326
41930CB00007B/919

* 9 7 8 3 7 4 2 8 0 0 2 3 7 *